Easy Guide to Serging Fine Fabrics

Kitty Benton

The Taunton Press

Cover Photo: Boyd Hagen

Publisher: Suzanne La Rosa
Acquisitions Editor: Jolynn Gower
Publishing Coordinator: Sarah Coe
Editors: Eileen Hanson, Mary Christian, Ruth Dobsevage
Designer: Jodie Delohery
Layout Artist: Carol Singer
Photographers: Scott Phillips, Boyd Hagen
Typeface: Bookman/Optima
Paper: 70-lb. Warren Patina Matte
Printer: Quebecor Printing/Hawkins, New Canton, Tennessee

BOOKS & VIDEOS

for fellow enthusiasts

First printing: 1997
Printed in the United States of America

A THREADS Book
THREADS® is a trademark of The Taunton Press, Inc.,
registered in the U.S. Patent and Trademark Office.

The Taunton Press, 63 South Main Street, Box 5506,
Newtown, CT 06470-5506

Library of Congress Cataloging-in-Publication Data

Benton, Kitty.
        Easy guide to serging fine fabrics / Kitty Benton.
            p. cm. — (Sewing companion library)
        "A Threads book" — T.p. verso.
        Includes indexes.
        ISBN 1-56158-090-2
        1. Serging. I. Title. II. Series.
    TT713.B43 1997
    646.2'044 — dc20   95-29413
                                                CIP

For Charlie and Hank

No book becomes a reality without the dedicated expertise of the publishing staff. The staff at The Taunton Press has been enormously and universally helpful. I would like to thank them all.

But especially, I would like to thank Eileen Hanson for her early faith in me and devotion to this project; Mary Christian for editing complex technical prose and making it readable; and Ruth Dobsevage for her attention to detail, wording, and layout. All three have my lasting appreciation for their patience, humor, and perseverance.

Deepest thanks are also due to the quick mind, pleasant disposition, and never-failing accuracy of Eva Kui, who sewed many of the samples shown in the photographs.

Introduction

The serger can be intimidating at first glance. There it sits with all those dials, spindles, needles, and inner gears, like an ugly toad on your sewing table. But once you fall in love with it, you will recognize it to be the true prince of the sewing room.

My own love affair with sergers began when my children "outgrew me" and I went back to school in mid-life to take on the challenge of expanding a satisfying home-sewing hobby into a career as a professional designer. Part of my education was learning all about the specialized industrial machines. Some were scary monsters that clanked out buttonholes, some were intriguing puzzles such as the multi-needle shirring machine (with 45 needles to thread!). But the one I truly longed for at home was the overlock (or merrow machine, as it's still called in the industry), the factory staple that overcasts, trims, and stitches the seam all at once.

At the same time, about ten years ago, imported sewing machines hit the American home-sewing market and caused such a sensation that home overlockers, or sergers, soon followed as companion machines—much as automatic dryers followed washing machines. In the decade since, the creative energy found in home sewing workrooms has uncovered exciting new capabilities for the serger and triggered many added conveniences.

Why bother with a serger? Because it's fast! With a serger, you can stitch, trim, and overcast a seam in one step instead of three, and in less than half the time of a conventional sewing machine. This remarkable machine cuts hours of precious sewing time from large and small projects, and will often give you more professional results than a conventional sewing machine.

Most people associate the serger with utilitarian knits and sportswear, yet it has a much wider application. The beauty of the serger is how it can handle fine fabrics. The firmness of the grip between presser foot and throat plate will help you control slippery fabrics such as lace and chiffon, and the machine zips through tiny, accurate seams in delicate fabrics, making it ideal for labor-intensive dressmaking chores, such as making large circular hems on tiered skirts, and fine heirloom looks, such as joining rows and rows of lace insertion for a christening dress.

If you already own a serger, let me share my excitement and professional secrets with you to help you discover new ways of getting the most from your machine. If you are still thinking about buying one, this guide, based on years of personal experience and experimentation, will help you decide which features and threading variations will best serve your needs.

Each chapter in this book addresses progressive steps to mastering serging with fine fabrics, so whether you are a new or an experienced serger, you will be able to launch right into hands-on techniques that you can adapt to your own projects. You can go through the whole book for a complete course in fine serging, or, once having mastered the basics, you can skip ahead to the stitch treatments you can immediately apply to a garment.

Chapter 1 describes the advantages of a serger and how the parts work together to form stitches. It explains initial threading and tension adjustments, as well as optional features and accessories. You'll learn easy maintenance procedures and simple troubleshooting to keep your serger at peak performance.

Chapter 2 helps you to select compatible threads and needles for your fabrics, prepare the fabric for stitching, and take advantage of helpful products and notions.

In Chapter 3, you'll learn to master useful serger skills, including starting and finishing seams, and sewing curves, corners, bias areas, and circles. Then you'll learn basic seams, finishes, and hems for all types of fine fabrics.

Chapter 4 covers more specialized applications so you can produce elegant self-ribbing for fine knits, add tailoring touches to crisp wovens, create festive detailing for special-occasion garments, and seam laces for delicate lingerie and heirloom treatments. Four simple projects let you use your serging skills right away.

At the end of the book is a handy photo index that will help you to review, compare, and locate the finishes introduced in the main text. This section will boost your creativity with the serger because you will see at a glance the various treatments you can use, from utility seaming to special decorative effects and monogramming. Setting boxes tell you just how to thread and adjust your serger for the treatments shown in the photos. You will also see the decorative potential of fabrics, threads, and edgings and design them into your projects.

1 *Demystifying the Serger*

Learning how the serger differs from your conventional sewing machine is the key to helping you identify its advantages over conventional machines and its potential for fine sewing.

Like conventional sewing machines, sergers have presser feet, feed dogs, flywheels, stitch-length controls, thread cutters, foot pedals, power connections, and lights. But they have no bobbins! And that means no winding, no running out of thread, no spaghetti-mop tangles beneath the fabric or in the bobbin case.

Another important difference is the feed mechanism. The interplay between the serger's long presser foot and the narrow feed dog holds fabric so securely that it feeds evenly with much less intervention than a conventional machine requires. Accurate feeding reduces the likelihood of stretching and distortion, so seams have a uniform, professional appearance.

For everyday utility sewing, the serger's fully enclosed seam finishes are much neater and more durable than conventional machine finishes, and they don't distort curved areas such as bias seams and neck facings. You can quickly and accurately seam delicate fabrics and roll them into tiny hems because the long foot and narrow feed dog keep tiny seam allowances from snagging in the feed dog.

The serger's flexible looper stitches have "give," so seams are stronger and don't break when stressed or stretched in knits. You can apply a staggering variety of utilitarian and decorative stitches to any fabric, from gossamer silk chiffons to sturdy action knits, and to any task, from tiny heirloom seams to fast blind hems for draperies.

Sergers even chain threads without fabric (a handy way to make belt and button loops) so you can start stitching without placing the needle exactly at the starting point of the seam and you can chain off the fabric at the end of the seam without tangling.

How a Serger Works

Sergers work on a very simple principle. First the knives mounted on the machine neatly trim the edge of the fabric, then the needles and loopers overcast it with thread in a protective casing.

Anatomy of a Serger

Although there are many different models and makes of sergers, all have a shelf at the back of the square frame (on some models, a convenient carrying handle is built right into the frame) to hold spools or cones of thread on three, four, or five spindles, depending on the capability of the model. An extension bar raises each thread above the spools, allowing it to unwind evenly from the spool and feed smoothly into the primary thread guides without tangling.

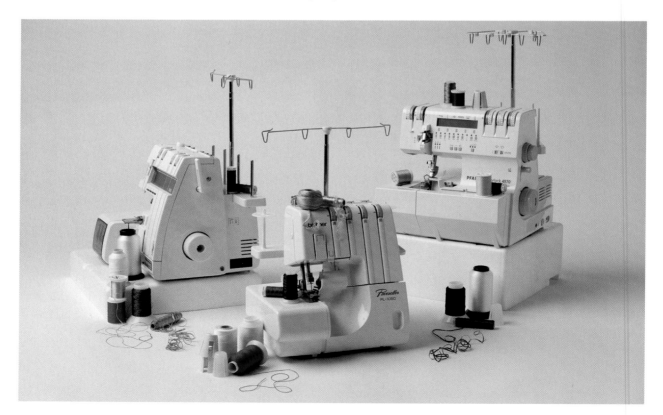

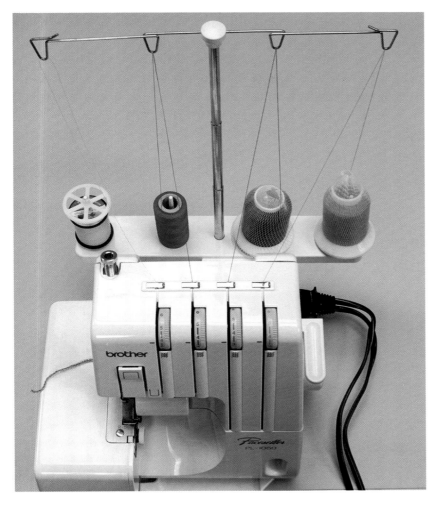

Front view of a serger. Threads pass over the extension bar and feed through primary thread guides before entering the tension wheels.

Two sets of color-coded thread guides control the flow of thread from the spool to the needles. The first (primary) set guides the thread from the spool to the tension wheel. The secondary guides, on the front of the serger, lead the thread from the tension wheel into the needle or looper.

Two knife blades trim the edge of the fabric as you stitch. In many models, the upper blade is mounted on a shaft above the throat plate to the right of the needles. The lower blade is housed in front of the loopers to the right of the feed dog on the throat plate. As you stitch, the upper knife blade moves alongside the stationary lower blade in a scissors-like cutting action. The moving knife blade is usually spring-mounted to maintain constant pressure against the stationary knife blade.

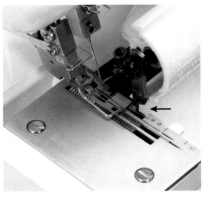

Upper and lower knife blades trim the fabric. (Presser foot removed for clarity.)

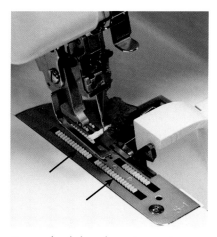

Serger feed dogs have two sets of teeth. (Presser foot removed for clarity.)

The upper knife blade can be rotated out of position when no cutting is needed.

The upper knife blade can be rotated out of position when you do not want to trim the fabric or when stitching prefinished edges such as lace and ribbon.

Serger feed dogs are similar to those of conventional machines, but they have two sets of teeth, front and rear. The teeth of the front feed dog guide the fabric under the toe of the presser foot, past the upper and lower knives for trimming.

The loopers move back and forth, simultaneously casting thread loops over the upper and lower surfaces of the fabric that interlock at the trimmed edge. The lower looper, positioned to the left and slightly below the upper looper, in most machines is threaded through the tension dial farthest to the right and moves back and forth from left to right. The upper looper, in most machines threaded through the tension dial immediately to the left of the lower looper, is located behind it, near the underside of the throat plate and needles.

The needles move up and down through the fabric as in conventional machines, but since the serger has no bobbins, the needles simply anchor the looper threads to each side of the fabric rather than interlock with bobbin threads to form stitches. When both needles are used, the left needle anchors the upper and lower thread loops on the seam line, while the right needle sews an additional safety seam. (When either needle is used alone, the unthreaded needle is removed and the safety seam is omitted.)

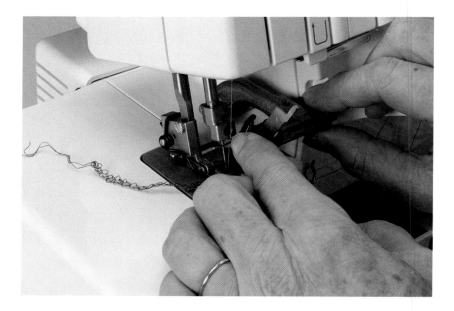

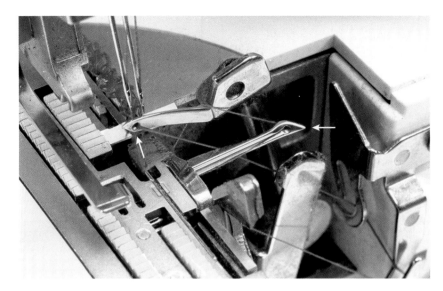

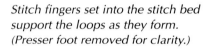

Upper and lower loopers cast thread over the top and bottom surfaces of the fabric. Needles anchor the loops. Either needle may be removed to adjust width of stitching. (Presser foot removed for clarity.)

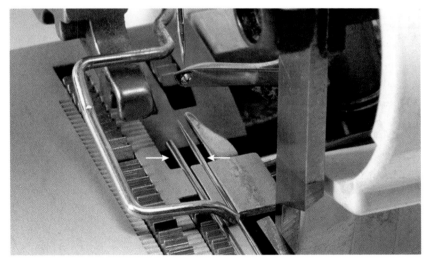

Stitch fingers set into the stitch bed support the loops as they form. (Presser foot removed for clarity.)

Stitch fingers, set into the stitch bed beneath each needle, support the thread loops as they form. Loops overlock around the two right stitch fingers when the right needle is used alone. The left stitch finger supports wider loops when the left needle is used alone and defines the safety seam when both needles are used together. A third. or overlock, stitch finger supports the loops as they interlock over the trimmed edge of the fabric.

After the stitches have been secured by the needles, the rear feed-dog teeth slide the stitches off the stitch fingers.

Getting the Most from Your Machine

There are seven variables that control the appearance and function of the stitches and give the serger its extraordinary versatility.

Fabric: The weight and stretchability of the fabric affect the appearance of the stitches (p. 26).

Thread: Choose threads that are heavy, light, smooth, textured, utility, or decorative (p. 28).

Thread tension: The degree of tension on the needle and looper threads will dramatically change the look of the stitches (p. 20).

Numbers of threads: For varying effects and depending on your model, all needles and loopers may be threaded, or selected needles and loopers may be left unthreaded (p.15).

Stitch width: Use wider stitch widths for more coverage, narrower for less.

Stitch length: Use longer stitch lengths for less coverage, shorter lengths for denser stitching (p. 22).

Cutting width: Adjust the distance between the trimmed edge and the needles (p. 21) to make the overcast edges either lie flat or roll into tiny hems.

THREADING OPTIONS

The greatest differences among serger models occur in threading options. Five-thread models are available with three needles and two loopers or two needles and three loopers. Five-thread models can usually adapt to four-, three-, and even two-thread uses, but since five-thread serging is most suitable for active wear and semi-industrial uses, it is beyond the scope of this book.

Needle Options

Three- and four-thread convertible models stitch with three or four threads. Both needles are used for four-thread applications, and either needle may be removed for three-thread applications. Remove the right needle for wider coverage on heavier fabrics. Remove the left needle for narrower coverage on lighter fabrics and rolled hems.

For tiny seams, remove the left needle and invoke roll-hem settings with the narrowest cutting width and normal thread tension.

Looper Options

In addition to using three- and four-thread applications, with two-, three-, and four-thread serger models you can bypass the upper looper and use either needle to stitch with two threads.

The photo below shows some of the different looks you can achieve by changing the threading setup on the serger (see the chart below for particulars). The top sample in each color was stitched with the roll-hem setting, yielding a narrower stitch; the bottom sample was stitched with the overlock finger slid into position, yielding a wider stitch.

You can change the look of your stitching by how you thread the serger. The setups that produced these stitches are described in the chart below.

Sample Color	Left Needle	Right Needle	Upper Looper	Lower Looper
White	removed	x	bypassed	x
Blue	removed	x	x	x
Brown	x	removed	x	x
Pink	x	x	x	x

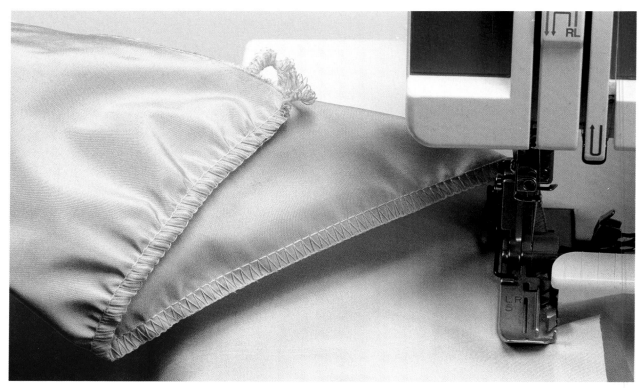

Puckering can be remedied by decreasing the differential feed.

Optional Features

Differential feed and adjustable pressure-foot pressure are offered as options on many sergers. Understanding how they work will help you realize the full capabilities of your serger or help you evaluate different models when making a purchase.

Differential Feed Because the serger has two feed dogs, the front and rear teeth can be set at different speeds. When the speeds are the same (dial at N or at 1, depending on the model), the fabric enters and leaves the stitch bed at the same speed.

If fabric tends to pucker, select a lower-than-normal setting. This slows the front feed dog, pulling the fabric under the presser foot, similar to sewing taut on a conventional machine.

THROAT PLATES AND PRESSER FEET

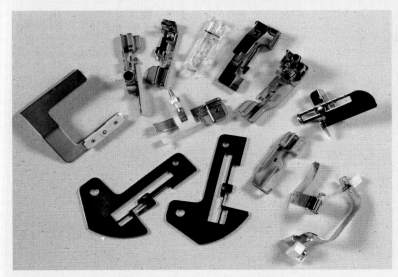

Accessories for the serger include specialized throat plates and presser feet for specific applications.

Various specialized throat plates and presser feet allow a wide range of applications such as roll hemming; delicate seaming; blind hemming; gathering; and applying elastic, binding, or cording. Some sergers are fully automated and require no change of presser feet or throat plates for these applications, while others require certain adjustments, sometimes including a change of throat plate and presser foot. Usually cost accompanies convenience, although convenience can be worth paying for in the long run.

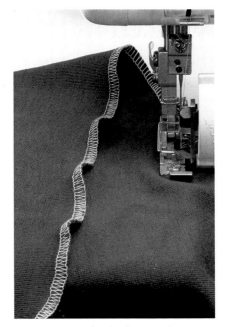

A wavy, stretched edge can be remedied by increasing the differential feed.

If the edge of the fabric is wavy and stretched, select a higher-than-normal setting. When the differential feed is set above normal, the front teeth move more quickly than the rear teeth, pushing the fabric under the presser foot and preventing knits and bias areas from stretching during stitching.

Presser-Foot Pressure Some models allow you to change the pressure on the presser foot. Lighten the pressure to accommodate thicker fabrics or to avoid teeth tracks on sheers. Increase the pressure to keep lighter fabrics from slipping.

Getting Ready to Sew

If you are new to serging, you are probably a little intimidated by the intricacies of the machine. Threading the machine needn't be daunting, though, if you take your time and follow instructions. As you practice stitching, you'll gain confidence and soon will be able to use serging in your fine sewing projects.

Initial Threading

Most manufacturers make threading easier by color coding primary guides and tension wheels. If you've never threaded a serger before, the task will be simpler if you select spools of ordinary sewing thread to match the color codes on your machine. Study the threading diagrams in your instruction booklet and use the long tweezers supplied in the accessory pack to help thread the loopers. Follow the threading instructions carefully. *Most stitching problems result from incorrect threading.*

Initial threading of a serger is simpler if you select thread that matches the color of the tension wheels.

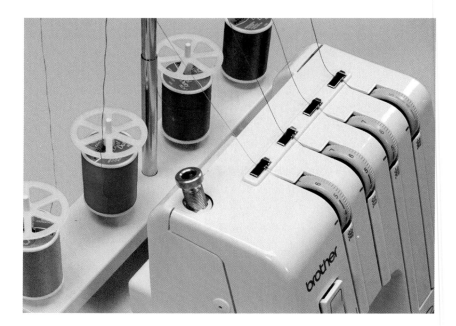

If a foam thread cushion was supplied, place it on the shelf beneath the spools. If you are using conventional machine spools rather than large cones of specialized serger thread, use the small plastic discs on top of the spools to extend beyond the rim of the spool and prevent the strands from snagging in the thread notch. If you are using the larger cones for your initial threading, use the net sleeves to prevent the thread from unreeling too quickly.

Starting to Stitch

Select a medium-weight, crisp, woven fabric in a solid color that contrasts well with your thread choices.

Set the controls for needle and looper tensions at normal range as indicated by your manufacturer, and select normal (or medium) stitch settings for length, cutting width, and other optional features such as differential feed and presser-foot pressure.

Sewing without fabric, chain a thread tail of 2 in. or 3 in. to prevent thread and fabric jams. Watch the thread chain to be sure it doesn't curl around and re-enter the stitch bed.

Stop sewing the thread chain while you position your fabric just in front of the presser-foot toe.

Resume sewing, letting the machine guide the fabric under the foot.

Chain a 3-in. to 5-in. long thread tail off the edge of the fabric before cutting the thread.

Begin and end your stitching with a short thread chain.

TIPS FOR GUIDING THE FABRIC

• Let the feed dog guide the fabric: simply use your right hand to keep the right edge of the fabric level when it approaches the knives. Place your left hand flat on the fabric to the left of the needles and let it travel with the fabric as it approaches the feed dog; stop to reposition every few inches.

• Learn to focus your eyes about 2 in. in front of the presser foot to give yourself time to make feeding corrections and adjustments. After the fabric enters the stitch bed and is hidden by the foot, it is too late to make corrections without distorting the seam or causing uneven stitching.

COMMON TENSION PROBLEMS

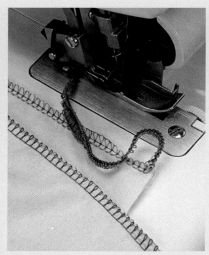

1 *If lower-looper threads straggle over the edge of the fabric and are visible from the top side, the tensions of the upper and lower looper are not balanced. Tighten the lower-looper tension in small increments before releasing the tension of the upper looper.*

2 *If upper-looper stitches are visible on the underside of the fabric, the tensions of the loopers are not balanced. Tighten the upper-looper tension in small increments, and release the lower-looper tension if necessary.*

3 *If needle threads form small beadlike loops of thread on the underside of the fabric, the needle threads are too loose. Tighten the appropriate needle tension slightly. If needle threads are too tight, the stitches will pucker. Loosen the appropriate tension dial.*

Properly adjusted serger stitches.

Adjusting the Tensions

Experiment with changing tensions and stitch lengths while chaining without fabric so you can clearly see the response to each change. You will see dramatic differences in the chain as it responds to each new setting. For best results:

• Follow the manufacturer's recommended settings.

• Adjust one tension wheel at a time, then check results.

• Make small, incremental changes.

• Check that looper threads interlock at edge of fabric.

• Make tensions of both loopers approximately equal.

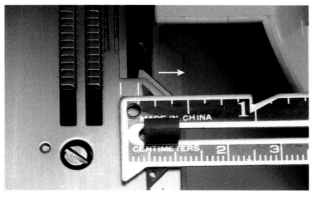

For the widest cutting width, move the blade housing all the way to the right.

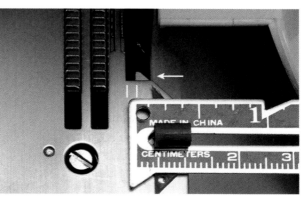

For the narrowest cutting width, move the blade housing all the way to the left.

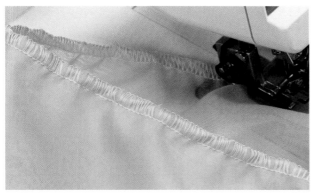

If the fabric twists under the stitches, the cutting width is too wide.

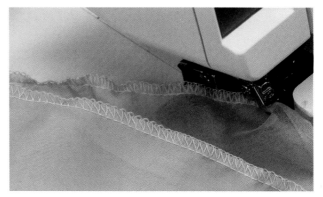

If loops form in the air rather than at the edge of the fabric, the cutting width is too narrow.

Adjusting the Cutting Width

The cutting width is the distance between the knife blades and the needles. It is controlled by a knob or dial that moves the whole blade housing outward to the right, away from the needles, or inward to the left, closer to them. You will need to fine-tune the cutting width along with the tensions to achieve the proper effect with each fabric.

If fabric twists and curls underneath the stitches, the cutting width is too wide. Follow the manufacturer's instructions to decrease cutting width, and watch the lower blade housing move to the left.

If the loops overlock in the air rather than at the edge of the fabric, the cutting width is too narrow. Follow the manufacturer's instructions to increase cutting width, and watch the blade housing move to the right.

REPLACING NEEDLES AND KNIVES

You may not be able to tell if a needle is dull, hooked, or bent just by looking at it, but a bad needle will affect sewing performance and cause threads to break more easily. Therefore it's a good idea to change needles frequently, as recommended by the manufacturer. Generally, needles will remain sharp for about 20 hours of sewing time. For a more complete description of needles, see p. 31.

To change a needle:

Turn the flywheel to raise the needles to their highest position.

Swing the foot out to the side for easier access to the needle, if your model permits this.

Remove the thread supply from the needle.

Loosen the screw above the needle and remove it, using tweezers, or a special needle holder if provided.

Insert a needle the manufacturer recommends, following the previous steps in reverse.

Small tears and frayed portions of the cut fabric edge are a sign that the lower knife blade has become nicked or dull. Most manufacturers include a replacement lower blade in the accessory kit. Change the blade according to the manufacturer's instructions.

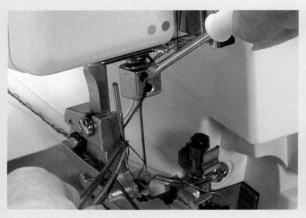

A tweezers and small screwdriver are handy for changing a needle.

To change a blade, follow the manufacturer's instructions.

Adjusting the Stitch Length

As with conventional sewing machines, the higher the stitch-length number, the longer the stitch. Gradually increase the stitch length while sewing to see the effect of wider spacing, then decrease the stitch length to see the fuller coverage of dense stitches.

Hints for Trouble-Free Sewing

Keeping your serger lint free and knowing how to unjam it when the thread snarls are important if you want your serger to run smoothly. It's also a good idea to perform periodic maintenance, as described in the machine manual.

Removing Lint Sergers make a great deal of fabric dust, which can become trapped in the feed dogs. Routinely replace needles (p. 22) and remove dust. If inadvertently sewn into the seam, a clump of lint can be a real chore to remove.

To keep the machine clean and lint free, frequently open the panel door and clean the dust away from the looper mechanisms, cutting blades, and feed dogs. A small brush for this purpose is usually included with the accessories, but canisters of compressed air, sold at computer-supply stores, are even better. To keep household dust out of the machine, cover it when not in use.

Unjamming a Serger If the machine jams, stop sewing immediately. Never try to force the machine or sew your way through; this could bend the loopers out of alignment and permanently damage your serger. If there is any play in the flywheel, gently try to raise the needle and cut the jammed threads away. If necessary, remove the needle from its socket. You can also open the front plate and use a seam ripper to free the jammed threads from underneath. Before you resume sewing, be sure that you have cleared away all stray threads, that the needle has not been bent, and that the machine is rethreaded correctly.

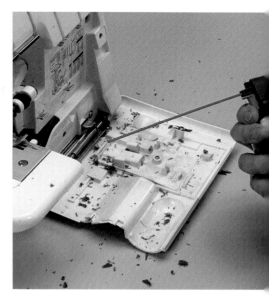

A blast of compressed air will help remove dust and lint from inside the serger.

When the machine jams, stop sewing and remove all thread snags with a seam ripper, as shown, or other small tool. (Presser foot removed for clarity.)

2 | *Fabrics, Thread, and Notions*

The first choice you make when planning any project is fabric. Eye appeal, function, and the styling of the garment you plan are the primary factors in your choice, but especially when serging, the decisions you make concerning treads and notions will be an important part of the appearance and success of your finished project.

Will you make fabulously tiny seams a design feature of serged lingerie, or highlight a pressed wool jacket with a bright edging? Will you have serged decorative sportswear details such as flatlocked seams or hems? Will you intensify the basic fabric color with harmonizing threads or accent it with a well-chosen contrast? Will you use thick threads such as pearl cotton or wooly nylon to highlight fabric texture, or shiny ribbons and glossy rayons or metallics to bring out the glamour of festive fabrics?

Even if you originally planned to use the serger for quick and efficient seaming, this chapter will give old hands and beginners alike many new reasons to keep the serger in mind when buying new patterns or adding flair to tried-and-true favorites.

Selecting Fabrics

All fabrics of all weights, whether woven or knit, are suitable for serging. In fact, with just a few twists of the dials, the serger can actually make some of the more "difficult" fabrics easy to work with. After selecting your fabrics, select needles and thread appropriate to the weight and weave.

Lightweight fabrics are woven from thinly spun yarns in fairly open weaves. Cottons, silks, synthetics, and some wools fall into this group. With lightweight fabrics, use thin needles and lightweight threads for construction and embellishment.

Medium-weight fabrics can be of any fiber (silk, cotton, wool, or synthetic) but the yarns are spun into heaver plies and more densely packed into the weave. Needles and threads should correspond to the weight of the fabric.

Heavyweight fabrics have the thickest yarns and often very dense weaves, such as twill or pile. Use heavier needles and threads to construct and decorate these fabrics.

Knits

Like woven fabrics, knits can be light, medium, or heavy, according to the weight and thickness of the yarn and the density of the knit. Knits can also be of any fiber, natural or synthetic.

The lightest knits are single knits, in which the wrong side looks different from the right and a single row of loops will appear on the edge of the fabric as it unravels. Double knits have two right sides and reveal a double row of loops as they unravel. Jerseys, matte jerseys, interlocks, ribbing, tricots, fleeces, sweater knits, spandex, Lycra, and panné velvets and velours are all knits that lend themselves to successful serging.

Lightweight fabrics.

Medium-weight fabrics.

Heavyweight fabrics.

Choosing Thread

Select threads for function and color. Utility thread colors for seams and seam finishes should blend into the fabric as much as possible. Decorative threads to highlight and embellish can be in matching or contrasting shades.

The same spools you use on your conventional machine can be used successfully on your serger. Such threads include cotton-wrapped polyester, all cotton, and all polyester. Specialized serger threads such as woolly nylon, two-ply polyester, and invisible nylon filament threads come on cones. Woolly nylon is a soft, comfortable, stretchy thread that is strong enough to be sewn under high tension, making it suitable for delicate seams and rolled hems. (Loosen thread tensions if you want the woolly nylon to fluff up as a filler thread.) Polyester and nylon filament threads also tolerate high tensions for rolled hems, and are thin enough to blend with most colors for less visible stitching.

CHANGING THREADS

The only time you need to unthread a needle or looper totally is when you are bypassing it. To change threads, simply leave the machine threaded, tie in the new color, as shown in the four photos below, and chain without fabric until all the new threads have passed through the eyes and into the chain.

A simple overhand knot is all that is needed to tie in new threads. Always test the security of your knot before threading it through the serger.

Stitching Knots Through

To stitch the knots through, trim the cut ends to within ½ in. to 1 in. from the knot. (Be careful not to trim the spool end, or you will have to retie the knot!) Loosen the tension wheels to let the knots pass more easily, and chain the serger without fabric until the upper and lower looper threads pass through the

eyes and blend into the chain. Since the loopers are thread-hungry, this will happen before the needle threads arrive at the needle eyes.

Even though the small eye of the needle rarely allows the knot to pass through easily, it is still worth knotting on. Just as the knot reaches the eye, cut the thread, pull the old thread out, and manually thread the new one. Resume stitching.

Threading Tips

• Use loops of ordinary sewing thread to help you thread loopers with threads that tend to fuzz, such as woolly nylon.

• If you are running short of thread, remember that loopers consume three times the amount of thread that needles do. Save scantier spools for the needles and fuller ones for the loopers.

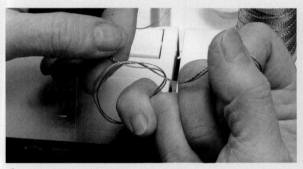

1 Tie in a new thread (blue) to the old (red) with a simple overhand knot.

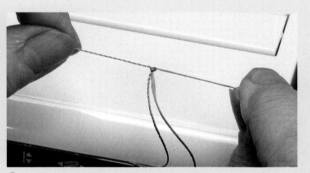

2 Be sure that the knot is secure before threading it through the serger.

3 Stitch or pull the knot through the eye of the looper.

4 Thread the looper with a loop of regular garment thread (red) and pull thick, fuzzy thread (blue) through the eye.

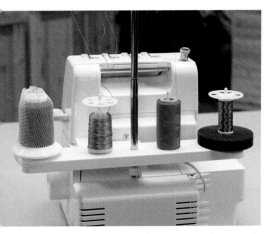

Decorative Threads

When it comes to decorative threads, sergers have it hands down over conventional machines. Thick threads that have to be wound by hand on the bobbins of conventional machines pass easily through the larger looper eyes. Since the serger spindles can easily hold entire spools, creative combinations of decorative thread can be chained into lengths to make custom piping and braid. Woolly nylon fluffs up to embellish a seam with decorative flatlocking, and raw edges can be overcast quickly with fancy finishes in place of hems and facings.

Experiment with mixing colors and types of threads for novel effects. Shown here (left to right) are woolly nylon (blue) in net spool casing, rayon pearl cotton (turquoise) with protective cap, cotton garment thread (red) on a 2,000-yd. spool, and (on foam cushion) decorative metallic thread.

Threads may be silk, linen, wool, metallic, synthetic, or cotton, and any thickness that will fit through the eye of the looper. For greater coverage, use decorative threads in the upper and lower loopers, alone or in combinations.

It is critical to ensure that decorative threads unreel evenly and flow smoothly through the thread guides. Some slippery threads slide off the spool and twist around the spindle beneath; others snag or fail to feed properly. For these difficult threads, bypass the spindle and place the spool in a cup behind the machine.

Decorative threads work best if they are smooth, strong, and supple. Avoid slubbed or irregular textures that might snag in looper eyes. Threads that break easily are not suitable for decorative serging. Stiff threads such as quilting thread or rug and carpet thread are also not suitable, since they won't feed easily through the stitching mechanisms.

For even feeding with difficult threads, such as this rayon ribbon thread, let the spool unwind in a cup rather than on the spindle.

Sometimes it is best to mix threads of different textures and colors. For instance, monofilament nylon or thin polyester are good choices for the lower looper to blend with a decorative novelty thread in the upper looper. Mix related shades of similar threads in needles and loopers to customize unusual or difficult colors. Neutral shades of gray or ivory are good basics that blend with many other shades to darken or lighten them; sometimes three colors can be blended for nearly perfect matches. When blending a seam, be sure to use the shade closest to your fabric in the needle.

Selecting Needles

Serger needles are somewhat sturdier than conventional machine needles, but they are sized in the same way: the higher the number, the smaller the needle.

The type of fabric you are using will determine the size needle you need. Heavier fabrics require larger needles, and lighter fabrics require smaller ones. For example, with denims, velvets, and corduroy I generally use a size 70 needle. With lighter-weight fabrics such as batiste, charmeuse, or organza, I generally use a size 90 needle.

Another consideration is the needle tip. For natural fibers, a pointed tip is fine, since natural fibers are twisted and spun to form the thread and are easily penetrated by the pointed tip of the needle. But synthetic fibers, being of chemical origin, are not twisted and spun but brewed in vats and extruded in long filaments. The strands deflect the point of a needle instead of allowing it to pierce them during stitching; this is why it is best, when serging synthetic fibers, to use ballpoint needles, which ease the filaments apart.

TIPS FOR CHOOSING SERGER NEEDLES

• Light fabrics: Needles must be small enough to stitch through the fabric without making holes. Needles that are too large will leave visible holes in the fabric.

• Medium fabrics: Needles must be strong enough to pierce the fabric easily, yet small enough not to make holes.

• Heavy fabrics: Needles need to be sturdy or they will bend and break during stitching.

• Synthetic fabrics of all weights: It's best to use ballpoint needles matched to the weight of the fabric.

Basting Techniques

Highly skilled professional sample-makers in the industry never baste at all and even take pride in using no pins. But sometimes we mortals really do need a pin or two, even for serging, which requires much less pinning and basting than conventional machine sewing.

When it is necessary to keep fabrics from shifting during sewing, you can pin (use caution), stabilize difficult fabrics with starch, or glue layers together with solid glue sticks, liquid seam sealants, artist's tape, or pre-glued basting tape. If you must baste, avoid basting on the seam line or within the seam allowance, because removing basting stitches might damage the serging and can be a time-consuming chore that defeats the virtues of the machine.

Pinning

The serger will not sew over pins! At best, either the pin or the needle will break. At worst, the knives will be damaged and the timing of the machine disrupted. When pins are called for, such as when matching plaids or holding very slippery fabrics, place them at least 1 in. inside the raw edge so there is no danger of one inadvertently passing through the stitch bed. On fabrics that may retain permanent pin marks, place pins at right angles to the seam line and be exceptionally vigilant about removing them from the seam allowance as you stitch; or consider other ways of securing the two layers, such as taping or glue basting.

Taping

Artist's tape, available at art-supply stores, leaves no sticky residue and is ideal for positioning sections that need careful placement, such as straps or pleats. Simply tape the area in question and remove the tape after stitching. Basting tape is concealed by layers of fabric, but artist's tape is always on top of the fabric where you can see it, eliminating the danger of stitching through it.

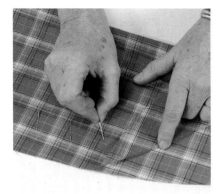

Place pins at least 1 in. inside the edges to be serged.

Glue Basting

Glues for basting come in liquid, stick, and tape form. Tape is pressed between the two layers, while stick glues and liquid glues are both applied sparingly along the seam line. Stick glue is the easiest type to control. If liquid glue is overapplied, it can cause skipped stitches or harm your needle. Most basting glues and tapes are water soluble—which is a benefit only if your fabric is washable. Tapes carry the attendant risk of being sewn through, making them much harder to remove, and they will not flex easily around curved seams. Test glue-basting products on your fabric to see if they will really save you any time or trouble. Sometimes pre-seaming at the conventional machine is the quickest and most accurate choice, saving the serger for non-construction finishing tasks.

Solid glues such as glue sticks and basting tape are easier to control than liquid glues.

Starching

Starching, though not really a form of basting, can serve the same purpose by stabilizing tricky fabrics, making them easier to sew. For lightweight fabrics and laces starch can actually bond two layers temporarily. Laces stretch like bias fabric and need to be stabilized with starch before stitching. Lay a protective covering over your ironing board (p. 35) and spray lightly. Allow the starch to settle into the lace before pressing. Stretch lace slightly as you steam with a medium-hot iron. A press cloth keeps starch from building up on the sole plate of your iron and prevents scorch marks on your lace or fabric. Similarly, if you are joining lace to fabric, starch very lightweight cottons to help support the lace during stitching.

Spray starch and pressing will stabilize lightweight fabrics and laces.

Other Helpful Products

When hemming difficult fabrics, bias tricot tape helps control the edges.

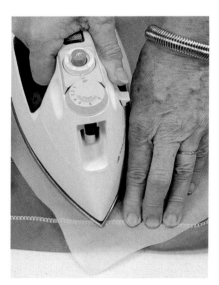

Fusible thread in the lower looper can be pressed to form a hem.

Notions counters are stocked with sewing aids that can significantly shorten sewing time and improve results. Those with the broadest number of uses are usually worth the investment. Grocery stores and art-supply houses are sources of other helpful supplies. Be sure to test any product on scraps before using on the actual garment. Check the labels for information on care, washability, and permanence.

Bias Tricot

Bias tricot is a tape of ⅝-in. or 1¼-in. width that comes in white, black, and several basic colors; it is packaged in rolls and sold as a seam binding to control fraying. In the serger it helps control stray threads that tend to escape when rolling difficult fabrics or bias areas during roll hemming. Serge decorative threads over the folded edge to create piping and braid; the tricot forms the seam allowance. It is strong enough to reinforce knit shoulder seams that might sag or stretch, yet flexible enough to let the fabric "give."

Fusible Thread

Fusible thread is sold on cones as a basting and positioning aid. For serging, manufacturers recommend threading the looper of the side that will be fused. (For example, if the wrong side of the fabric is to be fused, thread the lower looper and sew right side up.)

Cover every stitch of the fusible thread with a press cloth before applying the iron. Light fusing will be sufficient preparation for final topstitching; longer fusing at higher heat and more pressure may yield a permanent bond.

Water-Soluble Stabilizer

Lay fabrics that move or twist on top of water-soluble stabilizer and stitch through all layers. When the seam is complete, gently pull the stabilizer away from the stitching, as if separating perforated sheets of stamps. Rinse the remaining stabilizer out of the stitching with warm water.

A square of cotton organdy makes a good press cloth because it will withstand high heat and you can see through it.

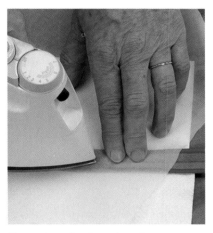

Water-soluble stabilizers support delicate stitching and are easily torn away.

Paper towels placed under seam allowances prevent imprints from the iron.

Prevent iron imprints of serged seam allowances by tucking folded strips of paper towel beneath allowances during pressing. Press as usual with appropriate heat and steam settings.

AN EASY IRONING-BOARD COVER

By serging ties onto a length of fabric, you can make an ironing-board cover that's pretty to look at and easy to change. Cut a width of fabric to fit the outline of your ironing board, allowing a 5-in. margin all around. Serge the edges, incorporating utility ribbon ties into the serging at convenient intervals around the edges. Tie tightly over your regular ironing-board cover and remove for washing or replacing as desired.

3 Skills and Seams

Once you understand the way a serger works, it is a short step to mastering the basic skills that will give you greater dexterity. Knowing when to stitch with the knives, when not to, and where they cut, combined with a thorough understanding of where the needle sews and which threading options to choose, will enable you to stitch accurately and evenly and be delighted with your results.

The speed of the serger affects how you guide fabric into it. Understanding what to expect and knowing the right ways to position your hands help you to gain control and manipulate fabric through the stitching process. It's easy to learn the basics, because they grow logically out of understanding the way the serger works. Once learned, they become the foundation for specific applications such as seams, interior finishes, and hems.

This section introduces basic skills first, preparing you for a variety of common sewing applications as well as the greater challenges of curves, corners, and placket slashes. The section on seams, finishes, and hems then presents a broad overview of serger uses. Several optional accessories for applying elastic or blind hemming are suggested, as well as several two-thread applications. If your serger does not have these capabilities, you can follow the alternative methods.

Most fabrics and applications fall into a few broad categories, so that even if a specific application isn't covered, the basic idea behind all the techniques is explained so you can easily make your own choices of seams, hems, threads, and finishes.

Building Serger Skills

Sometimes it seems as if the serger requires a whole new vocabulary of words and skills. Knives and loopers, trimming widths, cutting widths, looper tensions, and differential feed are things we don't worry about at conventional machines. Overlocking, flatlocking, serging, chaining—no wonder so many people have never even taken their serger out of the box!

The secret to it all is a few hours of practice with easy materials and plenty of time to put the knowledge of what the serger does and how it does it into your hands. It isn't even necessary to try everything. Just browse through this book until you find an application that tempts you, then try it. You'll find that the serger is not so intimidating after all, but really easy and convenient to use.

Understanding Where the Knives Cut

Knowing where the knives cut in relation to the stitching is the first step in mastering the serger. Once you are certain that you won't cut away too much of your fabric by accident, you will gain confidence. A few moments of practice with a striped fabric will help build accuracy and control. At the beginning, focus your eyes on the knife blade, then gradually shift your attention forward to the toe of the presser foot and the fabric passing beneath it.

Most models of sergers now help you guide the fabric with indications on the toe of the presser foot that show the positions of the needles and stationary knife. If your serger lacks these, you can mark your own as you become aware of the relationships between the toe of the presser foot and the stitching mechanisms of the serger.

Practice your stitches and seams on scrap fabric. Stripes will help you guide the fabric in a straight line.

Cut a 12-in. length of striped fabric with a relatively wide stripe (a 1-in. stripe is ideal) and calm colors that will withstand intense focus without tiring your eyes. Select a medium-long stitch length and a thread color that lets you focus easily on the fabric beneath the stitches. Set the cutting width at its widest setting. Thread tensions and feed options (if any) should be normal.

At first, focus on the inner edge of the stationary knife blade (nearest the needles), then stitch until the cut edge is perfectly straight and coincides exactly with the edge of the stripe. Usually, when the cutting width is at its widest setting, the right edge of the presser-foot toe will coincide with the inner edge of the stationary knife blade.

CUTTING WIDTH

Cutting width is the distance between the stitching and the knives.

Narrow cutting widths are best for overcasting tiny seams on delicate fabrics and for flatlocking trimmed edges. Wide cutting widths are used for overcasting seams on heavier fabrics and for rolled-hem settings on lighter fabrics.

Moving the position of the blade housing changes the cutting width. The widest setting is shown in the photo at left; the narrowest is shown in the photo at right.

 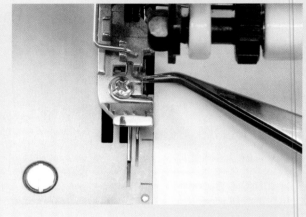

TRIMMING WIDTH

The trimming width, or the portion of the seam allowance that is cut away and discarded, is the distance between the raw edge of the fabric and the knives. The trimming width varies with the seam allowance and the location of the seam. When seaming and overcasting are simultaneous, sergers trim a preset distance from the seamline automatically. When you are overcasting the allowance of a seam you have stitched conventionally, trim the same amount of excess fabric from the seam allowance that you would with conventional methods.

Even if the seam allowance is small (or if it has been previously trimmed and altered), you should still plan to trim a tiny portion away from the very edge to ensure a crisp even edge and uniform overcasting.

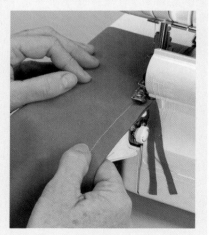

The trimming width falls away as you stitch.

With another length of the same fabric, rotate the stationary knife control to select the smallest cutting width, and stitch until you can confidently sew the edge of the stripe in a straight line, learning to focus on the toe of the presser foot instead of the blade.

Finally, with a third length of fabric, begin stitching again at the narrowest cutting width. Halfway through the length, stop stitching, raise the needle, and rotate the stationary knife outward to the widest setting. If you lower the foot and resume sewing while still guiding the fabric toward the narrowest cutting-width indicator on the foot, you will see the stitching veer 2mm to the right and into the neighboring stripe.

Mastering Where the Needle Sews

After becoming confident about where the knives cut, you can learn where each needle will sew. Again practice with the striped fabric, since it will show the accuracy of your stitching. Start practicing with both needles in the machine, then remove first the right, then the left.

The stitch fingers are couched in long grooves just to the right of each needle. Look just to the left of this groove to see if the toe of your presser foot has been marked to indicate the needle position. If you need to make your own guideline, mark the toe just to the left of each groove with a fine indelible marker.

Now cut another 12-in. strip of striped fabric. With all settings at normal, position the fabric so that the edge of a stripe coincides with the left needle position. Stitch, checking the fabric to be sure the needle stitches are aligned with the edge of the stripe. Make small adjustments in feeding as necessary until you can confidently stitch the length of the fabric without wavering.

Return the presser foot to sewing position and again stitch a length of striped fabric, this time aiming the edge of the stripe at the right needle. Similarly, stitch until you can follow the stripe with the right needle for the length of the fabric.

Mark the needle position on the toe of the presser foot.

The edge of the stripe is aligned with the mark for the right needle on the toe of the presser foot.

1 *Begin continuous seams by angling in from the right.*

2 *Complete continuous seams by angling to the left and stitching over previous stitches.*

Manipulating the Fabric in Special Situations

You will have all the basics down once you master techniques like starting and stopping, guiding the fabric, and learning to focus your eyes far enough ahead of the presser foot to make corrections without distorting the stitching. Now you are ready to tackle the more specialized situations that follow: angling on and off, avoiding the knives, clearing the stitch fingers, bypassing the knives, and making a cutout.

Angling on and off

Circular Areas Continuous seams such as cuffs, facings, or circular hems have no convenient beginning or end. To begin and end precisely and to stitch a smooth continuous seam, chain a few inches normally, then angle the fabric into the knives from the right **(1).** After the knives have begun to trim the edge, pivot the fabric into the normal stitching position.

When you reach the end of the seam, angle the fabric to the left away from the knives, and stitch off the edge of the fabric, sewing over the stitches at the beginning of the seam for about 1 in. **(2).**

When you need to restitch, angling in from the left lets you avoid the knives.

Avoiding the Knives

Sometimes you wish to avoid the knives until you have begun stitching. (Perhaps you need to restitch an area that has been previously trimmed, or you must seamlessly blend into the existing stitching.) To avoid the knives, angle in from the left until the fabric reaches the needles, then pivot into normal stitching position.

After blending into the existing stitching, angle the fabric again to the left, away from the knives, and stitch off the edge.

When clearing stitch fingers (p. 44) and angling off and on, remember that the knives begin cutting about ³/₄ in. before the needles enter the fabric.

CLEARING THE STITCH FINGERS

When you want to start or stop at an exact point, you need to clear the stitch fingers and swing the presser foot out of the way of the stitch bed if your serger permits. Then you can see where to position the fabric to start stitching under the point of the needles, or, at the end of stitching, to get the fabric away from the needles.

To clear stitch fingers without fabric in the machine (at the beginning of a seam):

Chain a length of thread.

Stop sewing and raise the needles to the highest point.

Raise the presser foot and swing it to the left (if possible).

Pull about ½ in. of slack in the needle threads.

Pull the thread chain behind the presser foot until the stitch fingers clear.

Position the fabric under the point of the needles as you would on a conventional machine.

Swing the presser foot back into position (if necessary), lower it, and resume sewing.

To clear stitch fingers with fabric in the machine (at an exact stopping point):

Stop sewing.

Pull ½ in. of slack in front of the needles.

Raise the needles to the highest point.

Raise the presser foot and swing it out of the way (if possible).

Pull the fabric back until the stitch fingers clear and the edge of the fabric is just behind the points of the needles.

Swing the presser foot back (if necessary), lower it, and resume sewing to chain a thread tail.

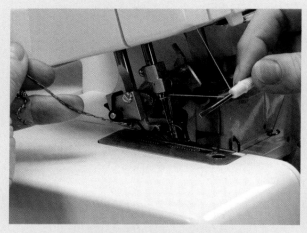

To clear the stitch fingers without fabric in the machine, chain, then pull slack in the thread. (Presser foot removed for clarity.)

To clear the stitch fingers with fabric in the machine, pull the fabric back until the fingers clear. (Presser foot removed for clarity.)

Bypassing the Knives Angling on and off (p. 42) is one way of bypassing the knives; here are two more ways to bypass the knives as you begin stitching. Both require clearing the stitch fingers.

Folding on

When the edge has already been trimmed, clear the stitch fingers and fold the fabric diagonally away from the needle at the point where you begin stitching.

Position the needle right at the fold.

Begin stitching with the trimmed edge abutting the inside of the knife. If you want to neaten the edge after you begin stitching, just swing the fabric slightly to the right in the path of the knife.

Making a Cutout

With scissors, cut out some of the seam allowance on your starting edge. To start in the middle of a circular edge such as a large hem, cut the trimming width from the edge for about 2 in.

Clear the stitch fingers and position the fabric under the needles right at the beginning of the cutout (**1**) with the trimmed edge abutting the inside of the knife.

At the end of the circle, stop where stitching begins, clear the stitch fingers, and chain off so the stitching is continuous (**2**), with no gap between beginning and end and no overlap.

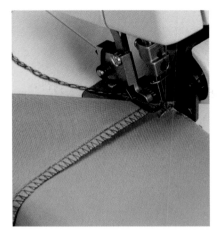

When the edge has been trimmed, clear the fingers and fold the fabric diagonally away from the needle. (Presser foot removed for clarity.)

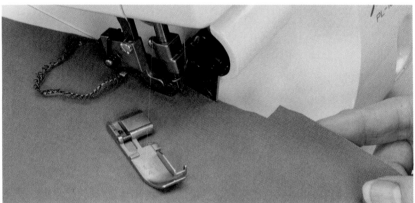

1 *To begin serging a circular edge, position the needle at the beginning of the cutout. (Presser foot removed for clarity.)*

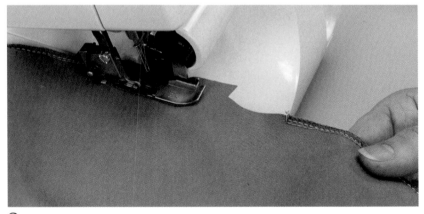

2 *End a circular edge by clearing the stitch fingers and chaining off so stitching is continuous.*

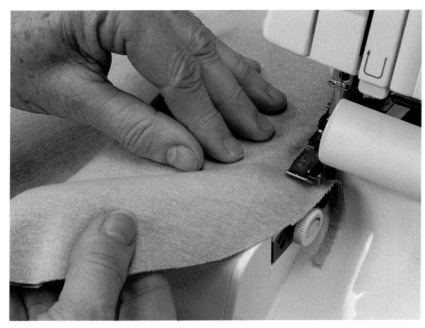

To follow an outside curve, press down with your fingers, creating a pivot point.

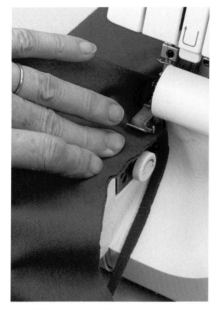

To follow an inside curve, push the fabric toward the knife as you stitch.

To seam outside corners with two needles, place the hand-trimmed portion of the second side flush against the knives.

Following Outside Curves

Watch the knives carefully while sewing curved seams, because the fabric will not pivot in the grip of the presser foot. Press the fabric down on the deck of the serger, to the left of the needles, to create a central pivot point; allow the raw edge to travel at the speed of the feed dog.

Following Inside Curves

On inside curves, the challenge is to keep the trimmed edge from curving away from the knife. Push the fabric slightly toward the knife as you stitch, being sure the trimmed edge stays flush against the blade. Slight puckering to the left of the needle is normal. Don't worry—it will vanish as the seam is stitched.

Turning Outside Corners

Outside corners may be seamed using two needles or decoratively stitched continuously, using one needle.

Two-needle non-continuous method

With your scissors, hand-trim the trimming width from the first 2 in. of the seam allowance on the second side.

Sew completely off the first side, cut the threads, and start the second side as if it were a new seam, stitching over the overlocked edge of the first side and keeping the hand-trimmed edge of the corner flush against the knives for the length of the cutout.

Using a large-eyed hand-sewing needle, run the thread tail back through the stitching to conceal it.

One-needle method for continuous decorative stitching

Remove one of the needles according to the desired width of the stitching.

BUILDING SKILLS AT CORNERS

Learning to stitch corners can be tricky. It may take several tries before you can successfully stitch a continuous corner without pulling the edge into the stitching at the beginning of the second side (by starting too far away from the needles) or without creating thread loops that extend beyond the fabric (by pulling too much thread slack when clearing the stitch fingers).

When stitching corners, adjust the cutting width for each fabric. Adjust to as narrow a width as possible that keeps stitches from falling off the edge. You also need to select the right needle combination.

Use two needles for:

• Gradual curves

• Outside corners (using the non-continuous stitch method, which is described on p. 46)

Use one needle for :

• Extremely curved areas

• Seams at conventional machine, then serge-overcast with one needle

• Slashes

•Inside curves

Use the left needle only for:

• Crisp medium- and heavyweight fabrics that will support wider decorative stitching and heavier thread

Use the right needle only for:

• All fabrics, particularly delicates

• Overcast prestitched interior corners

• All other corners and curves

Trim 2 in. of seam allowance from the second side.

Stitch the first side, stopping exactly when the needle comes to the edge of the fabric.

Lift the presser foot and clear the stitch fingers (p. 44).

Position the second side directly under the point of the needle, align the trimmed portion of the seam allowance flush against the knife blade, and resume stitching.

Overcasting Seamed Inside Corners Slash the seam allowance to the corner and spread the fabric flat into a straight line. As you spread the slash, pleats will form in the fabric.

Distribute this fullness evenly on either side of the slash, and secure with tape.

Overcast the seam allowance, stitching in a straight line right over the slash.

To stitch decorative corners continuously with one needle, hand-trim the first 2 in. before starting the second side.

To overcast seamed inside corners, slash to the corner, pleat the fabric, and spread the fabric into a straight line.

PLACKETS

Plackets are like inside corners with a hairpin turn. Using the slash-and-spread technique for inside corners, plackets can be serged with decorative thread for an attractive finish. Slash the fabric as the pattern directs, spread into a straight line, select minimal cutting width to support the decorative thread, and overcast in a straight line, keeping the edge of the slash flush against the knife during stitching.

Precision work like edging a lingerie placket with lace is simple with water-soluble stabilizer (p. 35) and artist's tape:

Slash and spread the placket, and tape it to the stabilizer with right side up.

Lay the lace wrong side up in a straight line on top of the spread placket, aligning the lace with the raw edge at the placket point and $\frac{1}{4}$ in. inside the raw edge at the top of the opening. Secure the lace with tape.

Set the machine for roll hemming (p. 62) and stitch, removing strips of tape as they reach the presser foot. (For instructions on how to overlock plackets or inside corners, refer to p. 47.)

Plackets can be finished by using the inside-corner technique (p. 47).

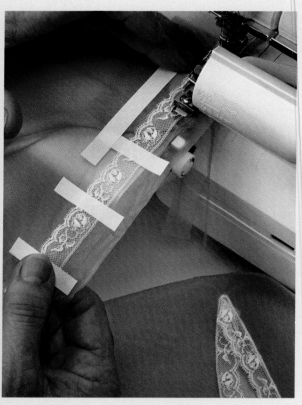

Even delicate plackets like this lingerie placket may be edged with lace using the inside-corner technique. Do not stitch over the tape that holds the lace in place; remove each piece as you come to it.

Sewing Taut

If the fabric tends to pucker during stitching, invoke the differential feed option (using settings below normal) or pull the fabric taut under the needle with both hands, being careful not to slow the natural feed of the fabric. Be sure to keep sewing speed even and regular to avoid uneven stitches.

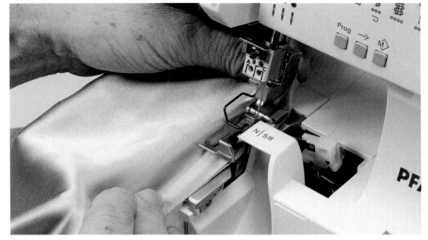

Use both hands to pull the fabric taut under the needle.

Machine Easing

When fabric has a tendency to stretch, invoke the differential feed option (using settings above normal), or duplicate its effect manually by placing your finger or a tool such as a screwdriver blade flush against the heel of the presser foot. Allow the fabric to pile up against the restriction as you stitch, releasing and repositioning every few inches.

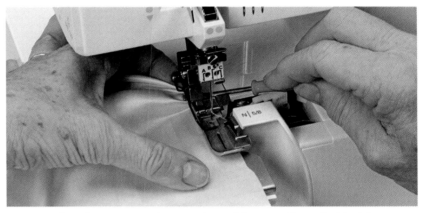

Use a tool such as a screwdriver to force fabric to pile up behind the presser foot to ease fabric or prevent stretching.

Holding Grain

The long foot and feed dog have a tendency to distort stretchy areas of grain such as bias, circular, or diagonal seams. To prevent this, "hold grain" as you sew. Press the fabric to the deck of the serger with your right hand and keep your eye on the weave to be sure threads are crossing at right angles as the fabric enters the presser foot. The seam allowance may appear slightly rippled, but the presser foot will flatten it again during stitching.

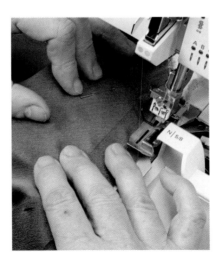

Hold grain by pressing the fabric to the deck of the serger with the right hand.

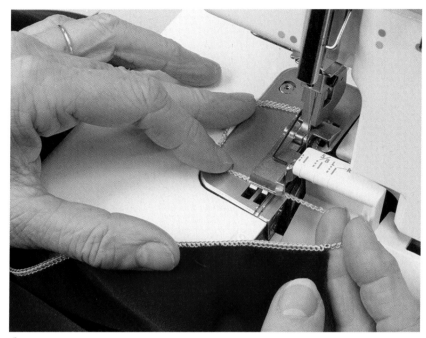

Ending Seams

At the end of the seam, cut the thread tail using scissors or the built-in knife behind the presser foot; or chain it around to the sewing position and stitch it past the knives **(1).**

If the end of the seam will not be crossed by another seam or secured in a hem or facing, you must prevent the stitches from fraying. The best way is to thread a large-eyed needle with the thread tail and run it back through the stitching **(2).**

Threads can also be secured with liquid seam sealant, available at notions counters. Apply a small bead, spread it with the point of a pin, and allow it to dry before cutting the threads.

Alternatively, the thread can be knotted at the edge of the fabric with a figure-eight knot.

First, loop the thread tail back over itself, passing the end under the tail at the fabric edge and then back up through the first loop.

Now insert the needle through the loop next to the fabric while you tighten the knot to settle it right at the fabric edge **(3).**

1 *Cut a thread tail by chaining it around to sewing position and stitching over it.*

2 *To prevent fraying, run the thread tail back through the stitching using a large-eyed needle.*

3 *Form a figure-eight knot to secure a thread tail.*

Overstitching at the Start of a Seam

Because overstitching creates a thick ridge of double stitching, it is the least satisfactory method for securing thread tails on fine fabrics, but it is acceptable in certain areas.

At the beginning of the seam, bring the thread tail forward just as the needles enter the fabric.

Position the tail so the needles will sew over it as they overcast.

Swing the tail in front of the knives and let it fall away after an inch or so.

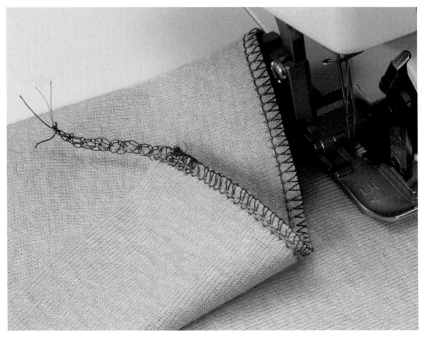

Overstitching the thread tail at the beginning of the stitching works on sturdy fabrics.

Overstitching at the End of a Seam

Follow this method if it is necessary to stitch the tail at the end of the seam.

Clear the stitch fingers just at the moment when the needles stitch off the fabric.

Flip the fabric and position it as if you were at the start of the seam.

Stitch backward for an inch or two and fold off.

Clip the final tail close to the seam allowance.

Overstitching the thread tail at the end of the stitching can be done by clearing the stitch fingers, then flipping the fabric over.

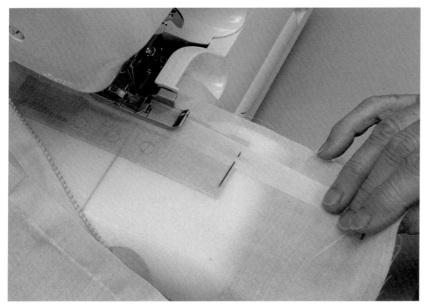

To flatlock a casing, make an S-fold in the fabric and serge wrong side up with a single needle.

A safety pin at right angles to the seam prevents the free end of the elastic from pulling through the casing.

Sewing Elastic

There are several methods for applying elastic at the serger; the one you choose depends on your personal preference and the function of the garment. You can flatlock a casing, overlock lingerie elastic directly to the fabric, or use an elastic applicator foot, available as an accessory for most sergers. Methods that don't involve stretching the elastic onto the fabric during stitching, such as the overlocked casing, give the most predictable results.

Flatlocking the Casing

Fold the casing allowance to the inside and refold the fabric with an S-fold. The folded fabric will resemble a tuck that overlaps the seamline into the seam allowance by a scant 1/8 in. The raw edge of the casing turnback will extend about 3/8 in. beyond the fold.

Remove the left or right needle (according to the weight of your fabric and the width of stitching you want).

Set the serger for three-thread flatlocking by releasing the tension of all three threads.

Stitch wrong side up so the extra seam allowance of the turnback is trimmed away, the needle penetrates all three layers, and the right side of the stitch loops fall off the edge of the fabric.

When the stitching is complete, spread the seam apart and press. The small "flea ladders" on the right side of the fabric will disappear into the folds after the elastic is inserted in the casing.

Close the final seam after the elastic is in place.

RIPPING OUT

It happens to the best of us! Sometimes you can't avoid ripping out. Because the tension of serger stitching is so much looser than that of conventional stitching, you have to use a seam ripper to release the needle threads for only a few stitches, then you can pull out the rest, as if you were pulling up gathering threads.

When the needle threads have been pulled out of the fabric, simply give the looper threads a tug to start the uncoiling process. You may have to repeat this process several times on a long seam. Take extra care not to damage delicate fabrics.

When ripping out is necessary, use a seam ripper to cut the needle threads.

Overlocking the Elastic

Cut elastic to the desired measurement.

Overlap and stitch the ends.

Mark both the elastic loop and the garment edge into quarters.

With right sides together, pin the elastic to the garment edge **(1),** allowing the raw edge to extend a generous $1/4$ in. beyond the edge of the elastic.

Overlock the elastic to the fabric, stretching the elastic to fit as you sew **(2).**

Leave the knife engaged to neaten the raw edge, but be very careful not to cut the edge of the elastic.

Attaching with an Elastic Foot
Place the elastic foot on the machine and stitch according to the manufacturer's instructions. The attachment will stretch elastic evenly as it stitches. Pretest the gathering ratio (p. 54).

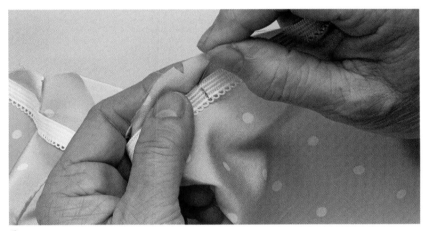

1 *Pin elastic to the garment edge, matching the marks.*

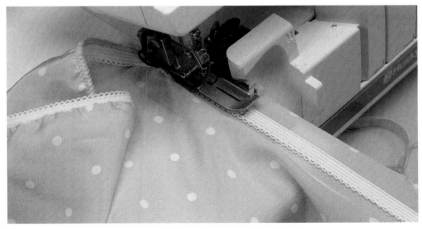

2 *Overlock the elastic to the fabric, stretching the elastic as it's sewn.*

DETERMINING GATHERING RATIOS

In machine gathering, the fabric is fed into the feed dog faster than it is drawn away. It bunches up beneath the needle and forms gathers as you stitch, saving you the step of later pulling up the bobbin threads.

Since this gathering is permanent, it is important to test your fabric before stitching to determine how easily it will gather and to see if it conforms to the gathering ratio of your pattern. Lightweight fabrics gather into smaller pleats, require shorter stitches, have many gathers per inch, and require higher gathering ratios. Heavy fabrics gather into bulkier pleats, require longer stitches, take fewer gathers per inch, and have lower gathering ratios.

Fabric grain must also be considered. Bias gathers are soft and drapey, fabric does not resist gathering, and the gathering ratio can be high without bulk.

Crosswise grain forms gathers easily, and the ruffles are crisp. Lengthwise grain gathers stiffly, forms less supple pleats, and creates the most bulk, so gathering ratios should be lower.

Testing Gathering Ratios

Cut a 4-in. wide strip of fabric to a length evenly divisible by 2 and 3 (such as 18 in. or 24 in.).

For 3 to 1 ratio: divide by 3 (a 24-in. wide strip should gather to 8 in.).

For a 2 to 1 ratio: divide by 2 (a 24-in. wide strip should gather to 12 in.).

For 1.5 to 1 ratio: divide by 3 and multiply the result by 2 (a 24-in. wide strip should gather to 16 in.).

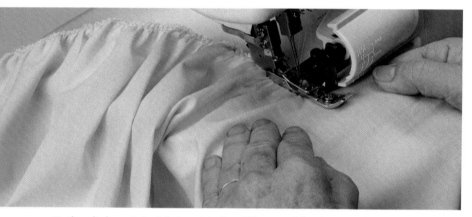

Gather lightweight fabric with the differential feed set to the highest setting.

A gathering-foot attachment lets you gather and overcast at the same time.

Gathering

Lightweight fabrics may be gathered without a special attachment.

Increase the stitch length to 3-4 (maximum length settings).

Increase the differential feed to the highest point above normal so that the fabric will be fed into the stitch bed twice as fast as it leaves.

Tighten the needle thread to secure the gathers. The roll-hem setting can be invoked to roll the top edge into a neat finish.

When gathering heavier fabrics, use a special gathering foot attachment available for most sergers. Follow the manufacturer's instructions for basic settings, and then test your fabric for gathering ratios, as described in the sidebar above.

Seams, Finishes, and Hems

The serger is surprisingly effective at seaming and hemming, as well as finishing. A variety of interior construction seams can be done completely at the serger; others are done in combination with the conventional machine. It is often preferable to make fine seams (such as French seams) at the serger, because the knives neaten the edges so effectively that no little threads pop out at the seamline as they can when allowances are hand trimmed the traditional way. Tiny hemmed seams can also be swiftly and accurately sewn in sheer fabrics, mimicking techniques used by skilled industry professionals, who use ⅟₁₆-in. roll-hemmer attachments on industrial machines.

Curved seams, such as armholes, that are conventionally sewn with straight stitching may be serge-finished in one layer after seaming.

Other seams may be pressed open and finished separately as appropriate, or "framed" with serging before sewing. Framing is particularly effective in stabilizing sheer fabrics to backings when two layers are to be sewn as one, eliminating the need to staystitch and overcast separately.

Sergers can save hours of preparation time in large circular hems. In wovens, you can either ease the extra fullness to fit or overcast decoratively edged hems; in loosely woven or knitted fabrics, you can make quick and easy blind hems.

The techniques that follow are organized to help you select the best seams, seam finishes, and hems for any project you undertake. (Serger setting charts for the techniques appear on pgs. 96-109.) Review these techniques frequently and perfect the ones that appeal to you, working on additional techniques as you choose. If you are still getting used to your serger, refer to earlier sections for help in threading, making routine adjustments, and preparing for stitching.

Basic four-thread serged seam; see setting chart, p. 96.

Basic three-thread serged seam; see setting chart, p. 97.

To avoid mixing used needles with new ones in the box, secure needles that have been temporarily removed to the inside of the front panel door with artist's tape until you need them again. When replacing needles, note that the long groove (which helps channel the thread through the eye) distinguishes the front, and the back is indented to accommodate the upper looper needle.

Seams

The basic three- or four-thread serged seam, the two-thread hairline, the bias hairline, and the two- and three-thread rolled seam are all one-step seams. The serger French seam is a two-step seam, prepared at the serger and completed at the conventional machine.

Basic Four-Thread Serged Seam The basic serged seam is sewn at the serger exactly as it would be at the conventional machine. With right sides together and raw edges aligned, stitch the seam from beginning to end, chaining a 3-in. to 5-in. tail at the beginning and end of each seam.

Basic Three-Thread Serged Seam Three-thread seams may be sewn on lighter fabrics in areas that do not bear much strain. Avoid three-thread construction for heavily stressed seams such as armholes or the inseams of highly fitted pants. Decrease stitch length and cutting width for lighter fabric.

Hairline Seam Hairline seams can be stitched with three threads, but are best sewn with two on very light fabrics (if your serger has the capability). For very fine seams, thread the needle with a thin thread, such as cotton basting thread or two-ply polyester. Woolly nylon is good for the loopers because it will withstand high tensions without breaking. Invoke the roll-hem

Hairline seam.

settings to produce very narrow stitch widths, and use the narrowest possible cutting width so the fabric will not roll. Decrease the stitch length and increase the tensions gradually if the stitches are visible from the right side.

Bias Hairline Seam Bias hairline seams are exactly like any three-thread hairline seam on grain, but the bias is so likely to stretch that the differential feed should be put to the highest setting.

If bias stretches even when differential feed is at its highest setting, stitch the seam on top of a strip of water-soluble stabilizer. Tear stabilizer away from both sides of the seam after stitching. Any stabilizer remaining in the seam will dissolve at the first

washing, but take care to use a press cloth to prevent traces of the stabilizer from fouling the bottom of your iron. For more tips on water-soluble stabilizers, see p. 35.

Two- and Three-Thread Rolled Seams For a rolled seam, choose a wide cutting width so the seam allowance will roll into the seam. Rolled seams may be sewn on lengthwise or crosswise grain. Bias and diagonal grains are difficult to roll neatly, as the bias threads escape from the seam, giving it an unsightly appearance. For bias edges, choose simple hairline seams instead of rolled seams. Crisp fabrics can tolerate a stiff thread, such as clear filament nylon, but use flexible threads such as Orlon or woolly nylon with softer fabrics.

Two-thread rolled seam; see setting chart, p. 98.

Serger French seams create narrow finished edges; see setting chart, p. 99. The preliminary seam is serged, then enclosed by a conventional sewing machine.

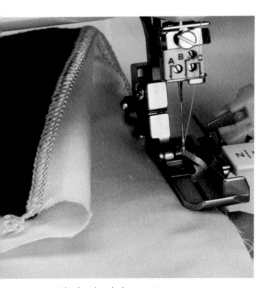

Flatlocked decorative seams are serged, then pulled crosswise until the stitches lie flat; see setting chart, p. 105.

Serger French Seam French seams, which completely enclose the raw edge in a preliminary seam, are quick and easy on the serger. Before you begin, make a sample: Choose the narrowest settings you can, and stitch a preliminary hairline seam. Measure the width of your hairline seam and add a scant bit of ease for turning to establish the preliminary seamline inside the garment seamline.

With wrong sides together, stitch the preliminary seam on the garment, as you did the practice hairline seam. Because the preliminary seam is never subject to stress, you can eliminate bulk with a stitch length slightly longer than normal. If your serger has two-thread capabilities, bypass the upper looper and thread only the lower looper with woolly nylon or another soft thread with a strong stretch that will not create bulk.

Press the hairline seam to one side.

Using the preliminary stitching as a fold line, align the right sides together and complete the seam with the conventional machine.

Flatlocked Decorative Seam
Flatlocked seams are overcast with three threads, using either the left or the right needle, depending on the desired width of the seam. The weight of your fabric and thread will determine which needle to use. Since flatlocked seams are strong design elements, be sure to test the effect on small scraps to ensure that the seam will be uniform, even, and worthy of such attention.

Loosen the needle tension generously so the needle stitches extend to the edge of the fabric on the wrong side.

Tighten the lower-looper tension until the threads are pulled into a straight line at the edge of the fabric. The upper-looper tension should be loosened slightly to allow the fabric to be pulled flat after stitching.

Select a narrow cutting width.

With wrong sides together and raw edges aligned, stitch the seam right side up so that the stitches are half on and half off the edge of the fabric.

Pull crosswise on the seam until the stitches lie flat. The decorative upper-looper stitches of the seam will appear on the right side, and the loose needle stitches will resemble a tiny "flea ladder" on the inside. If you prefer the flea-ladder look, stitch the fabric with right sides together so that the flea ladder will be on the right side. Test a sample of narrow flatlocking by tugging gently to be sure it does not pull away from the fabric.

Seam Finishes

Most of your serging will be for finishing seams that you have sewn at a conventional machine. You can serge each side of the seam allowance separately, or you can finish both layers of the seam allowance at the same time for small interior seams (such as armhole seams), where ridges will not show through to the outside.

When seams are to be pressed open, each side of the seam allowance should be serged separately before pressing.

Either way, you never again have to have an ugly notched seam allowance on the inside of your garment. When the pattern calls for trimming and notching small enclosed seam allowances, simply serge close to the seamline. In fact, clipping serged seam allowances is not recommended, because it causes the stitches to unravel.

Garment sections can also be staystitched or "framed" with serging before seaming. Most fine fabrics should be overcast with three threads, with the left needle omitted for a narrower stitch. Needles, loopers, and cutting widths should be balanced in all finishing applications.

Finishing Edges Together

Conventionally stitch the seam with the normal seam allowance. Then trim and serge both layers of the seam allowance simultaneously, stitching close to the original seamline. The trimming allowance will be generous, and the remaining overlocked seam allowance will be neat and flexible.

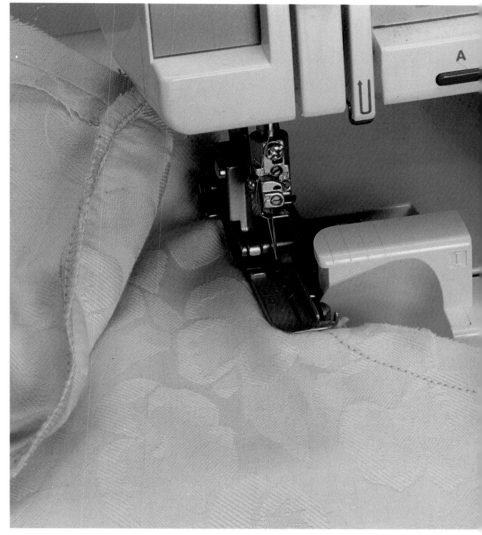

Narrow overlocking can be used to finish areas like armholes.

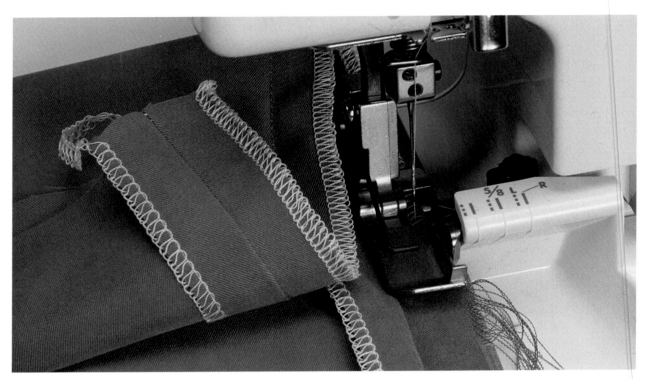

Single-layer overcasting; see setting chart, p. 103.

Framing with overcasting.

Single-Layer Overcasting

When stitched conventional seams are to be pressed open, overcast each side separately, trimming away just enough from the seam allowance to neaten the edge.

Framing with Overcasting

Single layers can be staystitched with overlocking before being seamed. Leave necklines, facings, and other enclosed seams unstitched, as the overlocking will create too much bulk. Chain on and off the beginning and end of the seam allowance and clip the chains close to the fabric. Don't worry about threads unraveling, as each seam will be crossed by another. When staystitching two layers together, pin the layers at critical seam allowances before serging, removing pins as you approach them.

Hems

Serger hems are just as fast, efficient, and convenient as every other finish on the serger. Hems may be blind-hemmed with or without an optional blind-hemming foot. They may also be clean-finished with single-layer overlocking for hemming by hand or with the conventional machine. Twin-needle hems, eased circular hems, and narrow shirttail hems (universally called "baby hems" in the industry) fall into this category.

Rolled hems rely on a narrow stitch and high looper tension to roll the cutting allowance into a tiny hem. The approach is the same as it is for a rolled seam, but a rolled hem, unless it is a receiving hem, has only one layer. Rolled receiving hems are used to secure lace edgings or entredeux to fine fabrics for lingerie or to incorporate stiffening mono-filament fishing line into very sheer fabrics to prevent drooping.

Stretched hems and flatlocked hems are decorative treatments that emphasize the wavy tendencies of bias areas and knits. Novelty threads such as metallics and ribbons look wonderful in stretched or flatlocked hems.

Two-Step Turned Hem Hems can be overlocked in preparation for final stitching at the regular machine or by hand.

For narrow topstitched or shirttail hems

Overlock the garment's lower edge.

Using the needle stitching of overlock as a fold line, turn up a baby hem and topstitch at the conventional machine with a single or twin needle.

For deeper circular hems

For deep circular hems, used eased overlocking. Overlock the edge with three needles, (generally omitting the left needle, as narrow stitching looks best) and ease the fabric by setting the differential feed slightly higher than normal. This will shrink the hem to fit the skirt after you turn it up.

Steam the hem into shape.

To finish, the hem can be sewn invisibly by hand or topstitched with twin needles.

See p. 34 for using fusible threads to baste hems in place.

Overlocking controls the ease of a circular hem; see setting chart, p. 99. Here, a machine-eased hem is pressed flat before final stitching.

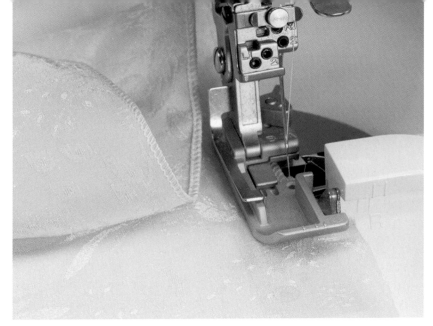

Basic rolled hem; see setting chart, p. 100.

Rolled receiving hem; see setting chart, p. 100.

Basic Rolled Hem Fine and lightweight fabrics can be rolled into hems that resemble those done by hand on French lingerie and christening dresses. The serger makes quick, accurate work of it.

Move the cutting width to the widest setting to leave enough fabric to roll. The stitch length should be moderate, but it is wise to test it for each fabric. Some fabrics roll easily and others have threads that want to escape from the hem. Surprisingly, increasing the stitch length can be most effective in controlling difficult fabrics, since longer stitches will permit the fabric to retain integrity, whereas shorter stitches tend to separate tiny cross threads.

Use lightweight, soft, stretchy thread, such as woolly nylon, under very high tension in the upper and lower loopers, with regular sewing thread under normal tension in the needle. Soft, thin, two-ply polyester also works well.

For a Quick Square Project that incorporates rolled hemming, see p. 89.

Rolled Receiving Hem
Receiving hems are rolled over the heading of lace strips for heirloom applications. Starch and press the lace and the fabric to stabilize both. If possible, bypass the upper looper and set the machine for two-thread applications, retaining normal rolled-hem settings.

Blind Hem

Prepare the hem: fold up the normal hem allowance, as your pattern directs, and press. Then fold the fabric back on itself, creating an S-fold (similar to elastic casing), and allowing the raw edge to extend beyond the first fold of the S.

Pin through all three layers at once, placing pins well inside the folded edge.

Blind hemming requires a precise start and stop. Clear the stitch fingers (p. 44) and prepare a cutout to begin stitching (p. 45).

Thread the serger with colors that blend easily into the fabric, loosen the needle tension, tighten the lower-looper tension, and moderately loosen the upper-looper tension, as you would for flatlocking (p. 58).

With the needle barely catching the fold, stitch with the right edge of the foot on the extended portion of the hem allowance.

Continue around the circle to the starting point, clear the fingers again, and chain off.

Unfold the hem and pull it flat, then press. The "flea ladder" may show in lighter fabrics, but will sink invisibly into heavier weaves and knits.

Decorative Thread Edgings

With the serger, you can make decorative edges that take the place of folded hems or facings. When using these finishes, remember to trim off your pattern's hem allowance. Choose a firm enough fabric to support the edge without buckling, use a novelty thread in the loopers, and set the stitch length to provide good coverage.

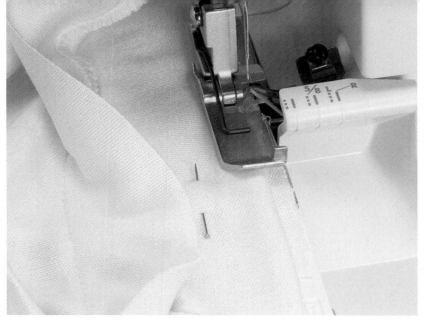

Blind hems are sewn wrong side up after pinning an S-fold at the hemline; see setting chart, p. 102.

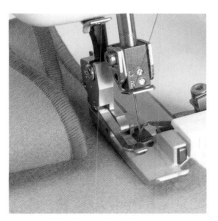

Decorative thread edging can mimic piping.

Lettuce-edge hem; see setting chart, p. 101.

Lettuce-Edge Hem Knits and bias edges can be stretched while overlocking to create a glorious ruffled edge that resembles curly escarole. True bias and the cross grains of knits stretch best; avoid fabrics that are too light to support dense stitching. Thread the upper looper with decorative or contrasting thread that gives good coverage, such as woolly nylon. Stretch the fabric as you stitch to enhance curling.

For a Quick Square Project that incorporates a lettuce hem, see p. 67.

4 Using Your Knowledge

Even though 90% of the time you might use your serger to finish seams, it doesn't mean that all the fun and creativity of serging are limited to the remaining 10% of specialized uses. The essence of good design is appropriate use of fabric combined with well-executed construction. If you are like me, you will enjoy the challenge of selecting the best possible settings to add to the professional quality of your work.

Since fabric is the key to technique, and there are so many possible settings and thread choices, I keep a swatch notebook of seam and hem finishes organized by fabric types. This way, if I haven't sewn with a particular type of fabric for a while, I don't have to reinvent the wheel and spend precious time experimenting all over again to find the proper threads, cutting widths, and needle tensions. I simply refer to the notebook to refresh my memory. Similarly, I organize more specialized uses of the serger in the same way. I staple actual swatches of stitched trims, decorative thread combinations, and successful experiments to index cards and make notes on the number of threads, tension settings, cutting widths, differential feed, and other optional settings or specialized attachments. This handy reference file reminds me of good ideas I had forgotten about and helps my new employees quickly visualize more creative uses of the serger than they may have encountered in factory settings.

In this chapter I share the convenience and cumulative experience of my notebook with you. The best seams, hems, and thread types for routine finishes (and the serger settings for creating them) are found in the Photo Index, which begins on p. 96. The more specialized and creative uses are grouped in the context of typical projects for clarity.

Working with Knits

Knits are the most fun of all to sew on the serger. Serger seams are quick and easy, and most knit styling is simple, so projects are not difficult to finish. The flexibility of serger stitches allows them to move with the knit without breaking, so every knit fabric can be stretched horizontally to become self ribbing for neckbands and cuffs.

Fine knits include all weights, from lightweight silk jerseys through medium-weight wools and cottons, to heavy panné velvets and velours. Any fiber can be knitted. As in wovens, the weight of the fabric depends on the thickness (denier) of the yarn, the number of strands (plies) twisted together, and the style of knit.

Double knits are knitted with two sets of needles and have no right or wrong side; single knits show the front and back of single stitches and have a "knit" and a "purl" side. Interlocks will not run, and the crimped yarns of matte jerseys absorb light and yield a dull, matte finish.

QUICK SQUARE PROJECT: LETTUCE-EDGE COWL-NECK SCARF

Choose a knit without an obvious right and wrong side.

Measure and cut a square of good-quality knit that measures about 22 in. (drape a tape measure around your neck to determine the exact size you prefer). If your knit has more body or weight, you might want to make a shallower crosswise rectangle.

Make a lettuce hem on each cross-grain edge (p. 63).

Serge-seam the two lengthwise edges using the four-thread serged seam for knits (p. 56).

Fold the tube in half, wrong sides in.

An Elegant Knit Top

Any dressy knit, such as silk or rayon jersey or velour, turns a utility tee shirt into an elegant knit top. A serged horizontal band of self fabric makes an elegant finish for the neckline and cuffs of a fine knit top. Choose narrow bands for crew necks and short sleeves, wider ones for turtlenecks or turnback cuffs for long sleeves.

Cut out the top according to the pattern directions. (To ensure proper fit, be sure to choose a pattern intended for knits.)

Thread both needles of the serger with garment thread and both loopers with a sturdy stretch thread such as woolly nylon. Start with the basic four-seam settings as indicated in the chart on p. 96, making adjustments as necessary to suit your fabric.

Sew the shoulder seams (reinforcing them with bias tape (**1**) or bias tricot as necessary).

1 *Reinforce the shoulder seams with bias seam tape.*

To determine the cut width of your self ribbing: For crew bands, determine the desired finished width of the band, double it, and add a seam allowance to both sides. For turtleneck bands and rollback cuffs, quadruple the desired finished width of the band (2) before adding a seam allowance to both sides.

Mark the cut width on the horizontal grain of the fabric, and cut a generously long strip. To determine the circumference of the strip, double the strip lengthwise and stretch it comfortably over your head or wrist. Pin.

Remove the band and mark the location of the pin to indicate the seamline. Add seam allowances.

Serge the center-back seam of the self ribbing. Fold it in half lengthwise, right sides out.

Mark the ribbing tube in quarters (the seam will be at center back). Mark the center front and back of the top neckline (3).

Distribute the band evenly about the neck, pinning seams and markings together at center front, back and shoulders. Stretch the seam band to the neckline using the cutout method (p. 45) to start and stop at the same point of the neckline seam. Press the seam allowance toward the garment.

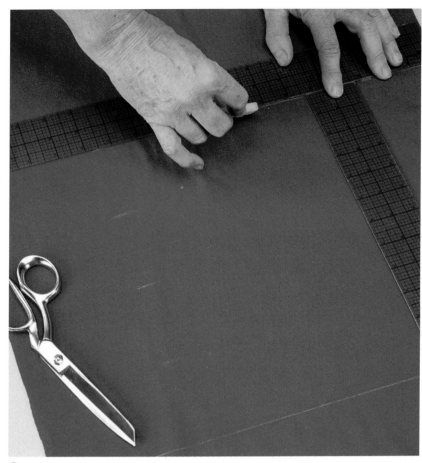

2 *Measure and mark the cut width of the turtleneck on the horizontal grain of the fabric.*

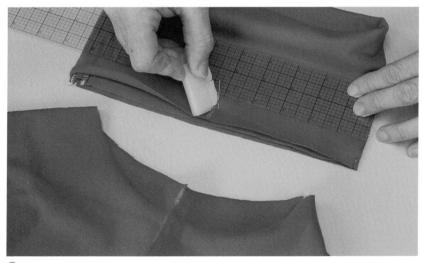

3 *Mark the folded turtleneck band and the neckline in quarters.*

Small ribbing areas like cuffs are easier to apply as flat pieces. Pin the sleeve self ribbing to the right side of the sleeve edge, raw edges aligned, distributing the sleeve fullness evenly. Stretch-seam the band to the garment **(4);** press the seam toward the sleeve.

Sew the sleeves to the armhole on the flat (before closing the side and underarm seams), aligning the appropriate pattern symbols.

Serge-seam the side, underarm, and cuff in one continuous seam **(5).** Use a tapestry needle to run in the thread tail at the wrist edge.

Hem the bottom using the blind-hem method (p. 63) or twin-needle topstitching at the conventional machine.

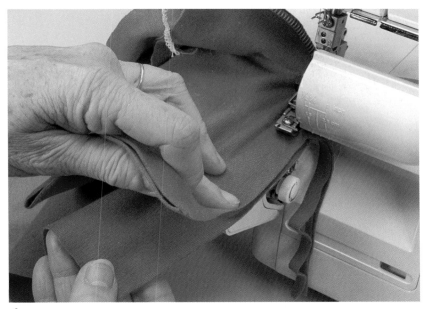

4 *Stretch-seam the cuff (or neckband) to the garment.*

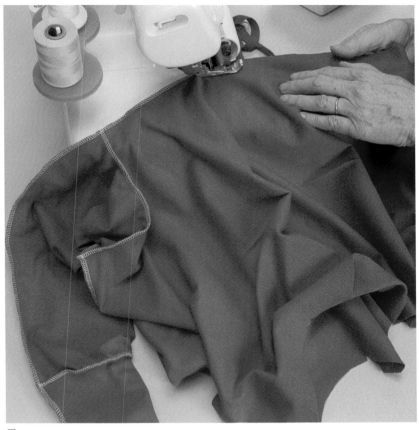

5 *Serge-seam the side, underarm, and cuff in one continuous seam.*

Tailored Finishes

Tailored detailing emphasizes the lines and seams of simple designs and adds surface interest to soft-finish wovens such as gabardines, twills, linens, tweeds, flannels, and broadcloths. The better the fabric and the simpler the design, the more the detailing will show. Use the conventional machine and the serger together for basic interior construction, then let the serger help you prepare your pocket edges or create tailored details such as tucks, decorative flatlocking, thread outlines, and custom braid for monograms.

Thread Accents

Textured novelty threads can outline seams or the geometric shapes of collars, cuffs, and pocket flaps. Treat decorative and novelty threads as part of the overall design, choosing them to blend, highlight, or accent colors in the weave or design. Match the weight of the thread to the weight of the fabric.

Tucking

Serger tucks are a good way to add details to tailored styles. They enhance the texture of the weave and, by drawing the eye to the direction of the tuck, underscore the vertical or horizontal aspects of the design silhouette.

Since the tuck is overcast, the looper thread will always show, and the thread selection becomes a design detail. Garment thread is customarily used in the needle.

TIPS FOR TUCKS

- Plan your tucking design and placement before cutting out the garment.

- Stitch tucks on lengthwise or crosswise grain.

- Sergers stitch right side up! Stitch all tucks in the same direction for a uniform appearance.

- Trim thread tails immediately before stitching the next tuck.

- Do not plan tucks too close together. The feed dog will not feed smoothly if the previous tuck is below the presser foot.

- Start stitching a vertical series of tucks with the center tuck; start a horizontal series of tucks with the top tuck.

- Press vertical tucks away from the center.

- Press horizontal tucks down.

- For wider tucks, remove the right needle.

- Since tucks are not construction seams, they do not need the extra security of three threads.

Lightweight two-ply threads blend well, particularly if the tuck is very narrow, and will emphasize the texture of the tuck. Novelty threads under high tension in the upper looper further distract the eye from the overcasting thread and add a color accent to your garment. For contrast accents, overcast with woolly nylon or decorative thread and stitch wider tucks to highlight the thread.

Most tucks are stitched in groups. Widths and thread detailing may be uniform or varied. See the setting charts on p. 104 for basic and decorative tucks.

To create a tucked fabric, decide on the width and number of tucks. Cut a square of garment fabric with enough ease to extend 3 in. beyond all edges of the pattern when tucking is complete.

To mark fold lines, press the fabric, starching it if appropriate. Position the edge of the ruler on the grain and lightly scratch a fold line for the first tuck with the point of a pin (1), steadying the pin against the edge of the ruler. The pin will fall between the threads of the grain and score the crossing threads. Avoid using too much pressure as there is a danger of cutting finer fabrics.

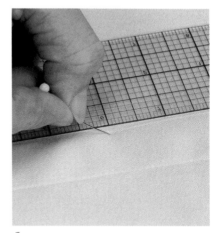

1 *Scratch the fold lines with a pin and ruler.*

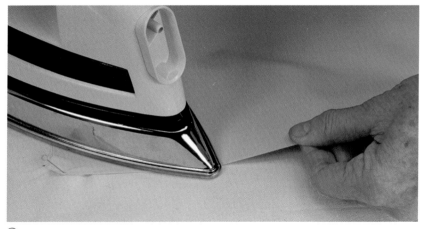

2 *A pin works as a third hand, letting you pull the fabric taut as you press.*

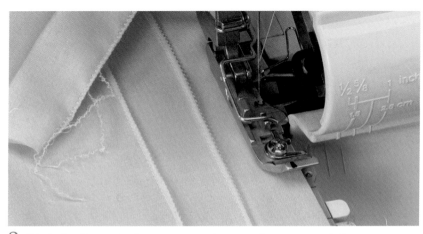

3 *Stitch the first tuck, then crease and press subsequent tuck lines.*

A pin placed through the fabric at a 45° angle secures the beginning of the tuck to the ironing board, enabling you to pull the fabric taut and press crisp folds **(2).**

Add contrasting or harmonizing textured thread such as pearl cotton to the upper looper. (See p. 30 for tips on working with decorative threads.) Increase the upper-looper tension by degrees until small beads of the thread form at the stitching line. Maintain normal tension and garment thread in the needle to hold the beads of thread, then loosen the lower-looper tension so the fabric can be encased in thread without buckling. A denser stitch length, such as 2mm, creates uniform thread beads on the stitching line.

Stitch the first tuck, then crease and press subsequent tuck lines **(3).** Continue in this manner until all the tucks are stitched.

When all the tucks are made, place the pattern over the fabric **(4)** and proceed to cut out the garment.

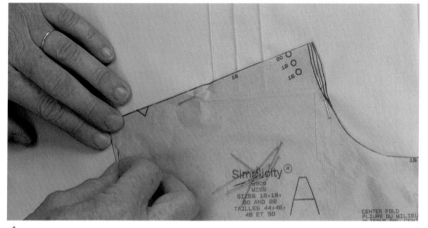

4 *Position the pattern over the fabric that has been tucked.*

Decorative Edging

Collars, cuffs, and pockets may be finished with the same combination of threads to complete the styling details. Since two-ply blending thread will not cover exterior edges, coordinated garment sections should be stitched, turned and pressed as your pattern directs. Seams should be trimmed to a scant ⅛ in. before turning and pressing so the seam allowance will fit entirely within the serging line. Serged edging holds facings in place without understitching.

Set the serger to match decorative tucks (see the chart on p. 104), or fine-tune your settings on a test scrap. Assemble the collar or cuff and stitch the trim before attaching the section to the garment. You must be extra vigilant not to pull and stretch curved areas as you align them in front of the toe of the presser foot.

Decorative Flatlocking

Any seam that might be embellished with piping can be flatlocked with decorative thread. Plan the texture and color of the thread as you would any design element: to harmonize, highlight, or accent a particular detail of texture, line, or color.

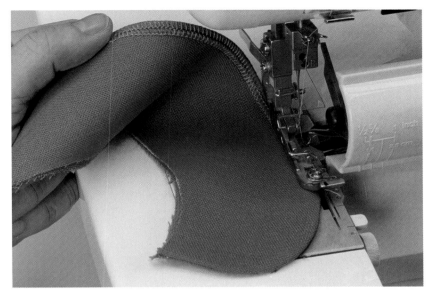

Collars and cuffs can be finished with decorative thread.

• Flat ribbon threads give good coverage and a softly gleaming finish. They can also be chained by themselves into attractive braid for monograms or other decorative outlines.

• Textured threads such as pearl cotton or woolly nylon yield matte finishes and less successful chained trims.

• If you like the way the needle and lower-looper threads appear to frame the decorative upper-looper thread, emphasize this with creative contrasts rather than blending threads. It is also wise to be sure the trim is washable if you plan to give the garment hard wear.

TIPS FOR FLATLOCKING

• Bypass the spindle if the thread has a tendency to wrap.

• Control the stitch width by using either the left or right needle, and turn roll-hem settings on or off. Be sure the stitch is wide enough not to pull out of the fabric.

Flatlocked decorative thread can replace piping in a seam.

To serge a flatlocked seam:

Prepare each section to be joined as your pattern directs. (The pocket band in the photo at left has been interfaced and pressed prior to flatlocking it to the pocket.)

Fine-tune your flatlock setting on scraps (see the top chart on p. 105), matching the width of the seam to the weight of the fabric and desired coverage of the seam.

Pin all the elements of the seam together and serge.

Decorative Chaining without Fabric

Chaining without fabric creates a decorative braid.

A few adjustments in stitch length and tension are necessary to chain decorative braids (see the bottom chart on p. 105). Retain the basic flatlock threadings and settings (see the top chart on p. 105), but return the needle tension to normal. Loosen the upper looper to make large loops (bypass the tension altogether if the lowest tension settings do not produce even results), and tighten the lower looper to maintain the shape of the braid. Increase the stitch length as necessary to keep the stitches from jamming on the stitch finger without the feed dog and fabric to carry them away.

MAKING MONOGRAMS WITH DECORATIVE CHAINING

Serging over a strand of fusible thread lets you bond your trim directly to the garment in any design you want. Holding the thread in a cup next to the serger (sometimes it's more convenient to hold the cup in your lap), guide it under the presser foot from front to back, positioning it directly over the stitch finger. (Temporarily taping the end behind the presser foot will secure it until it is incorporated into the chain.) Avoid threading the needles or loopers with fusible thread, as it can melt disastrously during pressing.

Lightly outline your monogram or design on the right side of the fabric with a disappearing marker.

Dot the outline sparingly with a fabric glue stick and arrange the braid over the marked pattern, pressing the glued areas with your fingers. If you are bonding fusible thread, protect the iron with a transparent press cloth (organdy works well) so you can see what you're doing without getting glue on the sole plate.

If you prefer non-bonded applications, hand-tack the braid in place.

Chaining over fusible thread makes a press-on braid that can be used for monogramming.

Fuse the chain in place, using a scrap of organdy to protect the iron from glue.

QUICK SQUARE PROJECT:
LINED EYEGLASS CASE WITH TUCKS AND MONOGRAM

Try out a variety of decorative tailored details with some lined eyeglass cases.

Cut a rectangle of fabric 10 in. by 20 in.

Mark and stitch the decorative tucks of your choice to embellish the case.

Cut a lining to fit the tucked rectangle, and fuse the lining to the wrong side of the fabric.

Fold the tucked fabric in half crosswise, and prepare and position a thread-chain monogram between the tucks, if desired.

Using your eyeglasses as a guide, trace a pattern on a piece of paper, using a ruler to ensure that the sides are straight, and curving the top slightly.

Place the bottom of the pattern against the crosswise fold of the fabric, and cut out the case.

Unfold the case and serge the curve of each top edge. Refold the case and, starting at the bottom fold, serge through all layers to close each side. For a quick shoulder strap, continue to serge without fabric for the length of the strap before closing the second side, this time sewing from top to bottom.

Time-Saving Construction Aids

Some tailoring details don't show on the outside of the garment, but are just as critical to the final appearance as the ones that do. Let your serger give you expert behind-the-scenes help for professional results every time.

Mock Hong Kong Finish
The Hong Kong finish is named for the island's skilled tailors, who finish the seams of unlined silk and linen jackets with bias binding. You can make a neat, easy mock Hong Kong finish with your serger. Threads that cover well, such as woolly nylon, are best in both loopers (see the bottom chart on p. 103); select the colors to harmonize, contrast, or accent.

Staystitched Pocket Seam Allowances
The serger eliminates all agony from topstitching pockets. Use any thread you like (garment threads are fine), and use balanced tensions for normal three-thread overlocking. Serge the bottom edge first. Press it in position over the pocket. Serge right over the fold when overlocking the two sides. Press, position the pocket, then edgestitch it to the garment with the conventional machine.

A mock Hong Kong finish adds a colorful accent to the seams on this jacket.

Inside Waistband Finish
Use the serger to make a neat, bulk-free waistband finish.

Interface the waistband and the seam outside edge to the skirt or pants.

Finish the inside waistband edge with balanced three-thread overlock, aligning so the serger trims most of the seam allowance and so the top of the overlocking will coincide with seamline.

Close the ends and turn the corners right side out.

Fold the waistband to the inside of the skirt, and position it so the seam allowance extends slightly beyond the waist seam and the tops of stitches are aligned with the stitching line.

Pin and ditchstitch from the right side through all layers.

Use the overlock stitch to finish the interior waistband and seam allowances of a skirt or pants.

Festive Detailing

Special-occasion fabrics range from lightweight organzas to sumptuous velvets. Sheers like organdy and organza can be handled like any delicate fabric. Browse through Chapter 3 and the Photo Index to find seam ideas. Tucks from the tailored details in this chapter also look great on crisp sheers, but avoid them in heavier pile fabrics or weaves that would snag.

Most other special-occasion fabrics are best seamed conventionally and finished with single-layer overcasting. You'll be delighted to see how the serger handles problem fabrics that fray easily and what quick work it makes of hemming big, full skirts.

Fancy Hems

Hemming the large sweeping skirts, tulle veils, and cascades of ruffles that are common in special-occasion and bridal wear can be a frustrating, time-consuming chore by hand or by the conventional machine. Let the serger do the work for you. Refer to pages 61 and 62 for how to ease a large circular hem or prepared a narrow topstitched hem ("baby hem").

The serger also allows you to create more elaborate fancy hems and finishes: You can thread-trace the edge of tulle veiling, roll supporting mono-filament into a droopy fabric, or embellish tiny rolled edges with decorative threads.

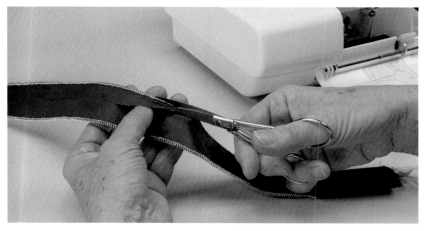

Use a narrow sheer hem to make your own custom ribbons! Cut strips of sheer organza or organdy and finish both edges with tiny folded hems to create custom ribbons for hair ornaments, sashes, or gift wraps.

Create festive ribbons in fabric to match garments by serging and trimming both edges of a strip.

Narrow Sheer Hem Some sheer fabrics such as organza and organdy fray too much for successful roll hemming, and you will need to make a narrow sheer hem.

Fold a small hem allowance.

Disengage the knife and stitch a 1mm hem over the fold. Be very careful not to allow the stitching line to waver, as too much fabric to the right of the needle will roll and cause uneven stitches.

Trim the excess fabric to the edge of the stitching on the wrong side.

Narrow Thread Tracing To thread-trace net and tulle skirts, set the serger for roll hemming with a wide cutting width, high lower looper tension, and balanced needle and upper looper tensions. Start with a 1.5mm stitch length; shorten it if the stitching looks too sparse, and lengthen it if the fabric tends to

bunch under the presser foot or if the stitching looks irregular with short ends of the net poking out of the hem. Garment thread may be used throughout or combined with woolly nylon or two-ply polyester, depending on the amount of coverage you want. The thread will stretch and cause the edge to curl slightly as you iron it.

Tearaway stabilizer supports metallic hem thread tracing on sheer tulle.

Wide thread tracing can be applied to net and tulle.

TIPS FOR THREAD TRACING

• The bias properties of net and tulle cause the stitched edge to curl when pressed. Set differential feed to .07 to intensify the curling effect of thread tracing, but be careful if you are trying to control the curling with above-normal settings, as the cut ends of the net will tend to escape and protrude from the stitching.

• The stiffening properties of metallic threads cause bias areas to curl in a similar fashion to monofilament fillings. Plan hems on the bias to achieve this curled effect or on straight grain to avoid it.

Wide thread tracing

To protect your hose from the raw edge of a net underskirt (or to match the edge of a tulle overskirt to a bodice), overcast a wide decorative border. Omit roll-hemming settings, select the left needle only, and stitch densely with a thread that covers well, such as rayon ribbon or woolly nylon.

Continuous thread tracing

To trace a continuous edge when stitching veils and headpieces or similar sections of veiling not crossed by seams, round corners in a large arc to create a modified oval shape. With the serger set at the narrowest setting for roll hemming (see the top chart on p. 98), start and stop the traced outline at the same point, using the cutout method described on p. 45.

QUICK SQUARE PROJECT: HAIR ORNAMENT

Measure and cut several squares (or rectangles) of fabric, each about 4 in. by 12 in. The more layers you use, the puffier the ornaments will be.

Overcast all the raw edges of each piece with thread tracing (pp. 79-80).

Layer the pieces together and hand-baste them together verticlaly through the center with strong thread and long stitches.

Mark an overlap line ½ in. to 1 in. inside one short edge. Fold the end in, and baste the overlap line to the center line. Repeat for the other side.

Pull up the basting stitches to gather all layers together.

Use your imagination! Trim fabric scraps with one of the edgings in this book to make quick coordinating tailored or festive hair ornaments. Or make custom ribbons (p. 79), and tie in bows.

Complete the project by hand stitching the gathered edge of the hair ornament to a comb.

Lace Appliqué

Lace appliqué is a popular finish for the hems, sleeves, and necks of special-occasion wear, bridal gowns, sleepwear, and lingerie. Prepare the lace appliqué as your pattern or design directs. Trace the shape of the lace onto the receiving area of the garment, modifying extreme shapes as much as possible. Finish the traced outline with a narrow, balanced three-thread overlock. Refer to pp. 46-47 for help with inside and outside corners.

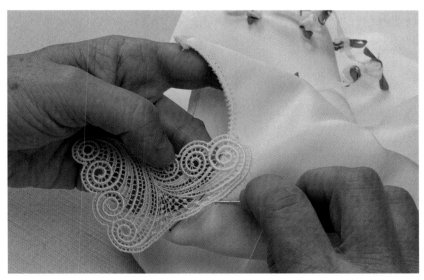

Prefinish areas that will receive appliqué with three-thread overlock.

MONOFILAMENT HEM

You can give a soft, filmy fabric a slightly wiry edge by hemming over monofilament.

Control the unruly stiff curls of monofilament at the beginning of the seam by taping the end in position behind the presser foot. With the spool secure in a plastic freezer bag or cup, stretch the filament taut above the right stitch finger, and chain 6 in. or 7 in. without fabric. Remove the tape after the first few inches to allow the chain to flow freely off the stitch finger.

Monofilament is so slippery that it will tend to pull out of the seam, but you can tape the beginning of the filament thread chain to hold it in place.

Mark the beginning of the cutting line on the fabric with a crease or removable marker to help guide your eye as you feed the fabric. Align the mark with the edge of the cutting blade and position the fabric right side up underneath the filament.

As the fabric begins to roll over the monofilament, use your left hand to ensure that the monofilament moves smoothly away from the heel of the presser foot without allowing the fabric to bunch up over it.

At the end of the hem, chain over the monofilament another 8 in. to 10 in. before passing it in front of the knife to cut.

Secure the end of the monofilament with tape until you stitch the crossing seam.

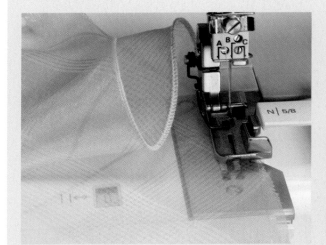

A monofilament hem can give a crisp finish to the edge of a filmy fabric.

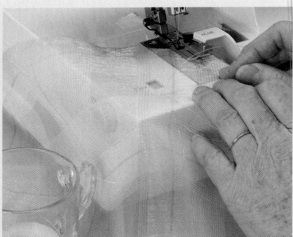

Control monofilament by securing it with tape at the beginning of the seam and stretching it taut as you sew.

Gathered Ruffles

Gathering long ruffles is one of those real chores on a conventional machine that the serger can eliminate for you. Let it chortle away, gathering as it stitches. The tedious chore of pulling threads in long edges is completely eliminated, and thoughts of breaking threads are banished. If your fabric is too heavy to gather with a long stitch length and maximum differential feed, you can purchase a gathering-foot attachment that will more than pay for itself after the first major project.

If you prefer softly draped ruffles to very perky ones, cut the strips to be ruffled on the bias. This consumes more fabric, but it will be well worth the professional result. Since the serger secures the gathers as it stitches, adjust your ratios (see p. 53 for advice) and test on scraps before working on the garment. It is also a good idea to cut some extra length to ensure that your finished strip doesn't fall short.

Seam lengths of the ruffle strip (if required) and hem the ruffle according to your design choice.

The serger makes quick work of a festive edge of long ruffles.

If you are not using a special gathering foot, increase the stitch length to 4mm and increase the differential feed to the maximum. If you are using a special gathering foot, follow the manufacturer's instructions.

Thread both needles, balance the looper and needle tensions, and stitch. The heading of the gathered strip will be neatly overcast, and the gathers will be attractively stitched.

Overcast the receiving edge of the seam before joining the ruffle strip to the garment.

Some gathering feet permit you to attach the ruffles to the fabric at the same time. However, this requires such precise measuring that it's best to gather separately and join later. Less ripping!

1 *Cut 2-in. wide bias strips, fold, and mark the stitching line.*

Bias Tubing

Bias tubing is a dreaded chore for many sewers. With the serger, tubing is ridiculously easy to make. It stitches and trims the tiny seam allowances perfectly, and since the stitches "give" when you pull lengths right side out, you won't get the popped seams that can ruin tubings sewn on the conventional machine.

Cut 2-in. wide strips of fabric on the true bias to the desired length, plus a few inches of insurance.

Fold the bias strip in half lengthwise, wrong sides together. Measure the desired finished width from the fold and mark a stitching line **(1).**

Adjust the width of the bias strip and the position of the stitching line to the stiffness, weight, and slipperiness of the fabric. Slippery, lightweight fabrics turn the most easily and make the thinnest strips. Stiff satins and brocades should be wider.

Measure the desired finished width of the bias strip and establish a fold guide to the left of the needle on the throat plate with a piece of artist's tape.

Select the narrowest cutting width, normal stitch length, and balanced tensions. If your machine has a two-thread capability, select this also to cut down on the bulk of the seam allowances (see the bottom chart on p. 98 for settings). Allow the knives to trim away whatever seam allowance falls to the right of the blade **(2),** keeping the fold of the bias aligned with the taped throat plate guide as you stitch and overcast both layers together.

2 *Use two-thread overcasting to cut down on the bulk of the seam allowance on the bias strip.*

Trim the top edge of the strip at an angle away from the seam. Push the point of a loop turner through the strip and secure the latch safety-pin style over the overlocked seam at the top (3). The hook should arch over the trimmed edge, and the latch of the turner should pierce the seamline about ¼ in. below it.

After pulling the turner carefully down into the tube to start the turn, hook the ring end over one of the thread spindles, backing slowly away to maintain even tension without allowing the turner to relax its grip on the starting edge (4). Use the tautness of the strip as a brace to free both hands so you can prevent bunching as you work the rest of the bias over itself. The overcast seam allowance remains curled inside as a filling. If you want thicker filling, increase the width of the seam allowance by increasing the cutting width and decreasing the thread tensions.

Secure one end of the tubing to the ironing board using a pin at a 45° angle so you can pull it taut. Steam the tubing to set the stitches and straighten the seam.

Bias tubing with the seam allowance rolled inside makes a very secure strap that holds well. Cut the proper length for spaghetti straps and sew them on as your pattern directs.

3 *Secure the latch of the loop turner in one end of the bias strip.*

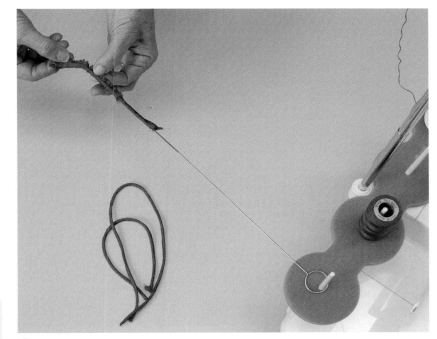

4 *Hook the ring of the loop turner over a spindle to help maintain tension as you turn the tubing.*

To make button loops, tape bias tubing over the pattern and serge it into position on the stabilizer.

Easy Button Loops Lengths of bias tubing can replace purchased cording or ribbon when a pattern's closings or design details call for decorative laces and ties.

Mark a straight line to represent the seamline on a piece of stabilizer. Center the buttons over the line, spacing them as they will be sewn to the garment.

Mark each side and the top of the button. Remove the buttons and loop the bias so that the markings are visible within the loop and the bias extends to the cutting line. The loops will resemble tiny croquet wickets.

Mark and cut the bias tubing according to the instructions that follow in "Buttons and Frogs."

Tape the cut loops to the stabilizer and staystitch them in position.

Align the raw edge of the stabilized loops over the buttonhole side of the closing, and staystitch to the garment just inside the seamline. Tear the stabilizer away before facing the closing.

Buttons and Frogs When dividing longer lengths of bias tubing into shorter segments for loop closings and straps, mark the measurement of each segment (plus desired seam allowances) and use the serger to cut and finish the tiny ends of each segment. Overcasting will slightly flatten the segment ends and make them easier to pin and stitch into garment seams.

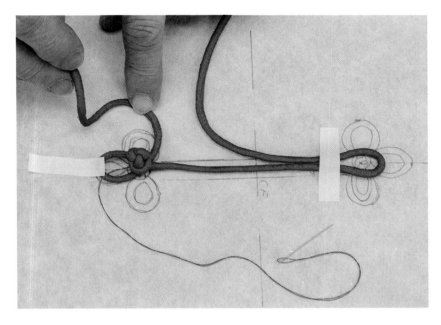

Prepare a diagram, and use bias tubing to create buttons and frogs in fabric to match the garment.

• For Chinese buttons, cut bias tubing 16 in. long and follow your diagram for the loop formations. The tubing seamline should be on top, and the loops should be relatively open while you shape them. Ease and shape the loops while pulling the ends to tighten them to form the button. Clip off excess ends and tack them to the button.

• For frog closings, keep the seamed side up and cut the ends on top. Secure the crossings with tiny stitches, taping and stitching the frog as it forms.

• To create more complex frog closings, draw your own diagrams. Similarly tape and stitch the crossings to secure the frog as it forms.

HERE COMES THE BRIDE!

Festive details are particularly welcome in bridal applications.

• Quick tiny hems can be used to prepare skirts and sleeves and trains for lace appliqués or other decorative finishes.

• Thread-traced hems are a good finish for veils and headpieces.

• Bias button loops are often used on bridal gowns for back and wrist closings as well as more specialized functions such as finger loops to secure the points of Juliet sleeves to the hand and skirt loops to lift the train out of the way for dancing.

A thread-traced veil and Juliet finger loops can be created with the serger.

Working with Delicate Fabrics

Delicate fabrics include lightweight silks, airy voiles, sheer chiffons, laces, thin crepes, and gossamer batistes. When lightweight fabrics are also sheer, the seam finishes are visible through the fabric and must be considered part of the design.

The serger is so effective and speedy at rolling hems and sewing tiny seams that you can rather surprisingly depend on it for most of your delicate-fabric construction chores. It sews and finishes hairline seams that are fine enough for even the most discerning eye, while offering sturdy construction security and enhancing airy fabrics.

Combine lightweight threads that withstand high tension without breaking and garment thread for construction seams or invisibly joining lace. Reserve the conventional machine for zigzagging tiny topstitched seams to miter corners and for staystitching difficult areas before serging.

Whet your appetite for serging delicates by making a really easy silk scarf, which is simply roll-hemmed on all four sides, before moving on to more challenging projects such as lingerie, sleepwear, and even christening dresses. Your serger will save you time and help create more professional-looking results.

QUICK SQUARE PROJECT: SCARF

You can create an impressive, nearly instant scarf from a preprinted scarf print (sold by the yard) or any solid color or appealing print. Some fabric stores carry bordered scarf prints, or try an all-over print of silk crepe de chine or chiffon that coordinates with your wardrobe.

Trim the purchased scarf panel or cut a square of fabric to the desired size.

Edge all four sides with roll a plain rolled hem (p. 62). Corners should be trimmed according to the instructions on pp. 46-47 and sewn continuously by clearing the stitch fingers (p. 44).

Run threads in neatly.

TIPS FOR CHOOSING THREAD

Your thread choice is a design decision that depends on the effect you want to achieve.

• To accent a color or create a contrasting border, use threads that provide maximum coverage, such as woolly nylon or ribbon, in both loopers and a dense stitch length, such as 2mm. Use garment thread in the needle.

• For minimal coverage to blend into the background color, select two-ply polyester for the loopers and garment thread or two-ply polyester for the needle. Increase the stitch length for less dense stitching, but not so far as to let unsightly threads escape from the rolled hem. However, since scarves are usually cut and rolled on straight grains, and silk is a close weave, stray threads will not usually be a problem.

• For custom effects or to harmonize with strong prints, change thread colors as appropriate to each side. If you change colors for custom effects, the ends must be run in (p. 50).

Camisole and Tap Pants

Any lingerie fabric is suitable for this camisole and tap-pants set: charmeuse, tricot, lightweight crepe-back satin, or voile. The only tricky part is the front shaping of the camisole. You can save time here by selecting a pattern without much shaping. Either way, the project should take no more than a pleasant morning's or evening's work, from cutting out to finishing.

With this and similar projects, seaming and finishing can be done simultaneously using hairline seam techniques that are fine enough for the most discerning eye, add immeasurably to the design effect of sheers, and offer sturdy construction security.

Transfer these techniques to a nightie or handkerchief, use your conventional zigzag to miter corners (pp. 94-95), and you have a lovely gift for any feminine celebration such as Mother's Day or a bridal shower.

Join preliminary seams: Using the bias hairline seam (p. 57), join the first side seam of the camisole and the center front and side seams of the tap pants, seaming nearly continuously. Clip the pieces apart after seaming, then press. Leave one side seam of the camisole and the center back and crotch seams of the pants open so you can complete the lace assembly on the flat.

Prepare the trim assembly: To create a strip of your laces, total the measurements of all areas to be trimmed. For the camisole and tap pants, measure both leg openings of the pants and the top and bottom edges of the camisole. Cut the lace strips to equal the total measurement plus 12 in.

Starch and press the lace before serging the seam. Rotate the upper knife out of position (1), and serge with the two-thread invisible seam (see the bottom chart on p. 98).

Staystitch the lace to the seamline at the conventional machine using a normal stitch length of 8 to 10 stitches per inch and a slightly relaxed upper-thread tension. To trim the bottom of the camisole and the legs of the pants, cut one length of the lace assembly to fit each leg opening and another to fit the bottom of the camisole. Serge as before; you may opt to staystitch conventionally or not, depending on your confidence and experience. Again press the hem away from the fabric and toward the lace to avoid bulk.

1 *Serge the lace with a two-thread invisible seam, with the upper knife rotated out of position.*

SAVE TIME BY WORKING IN UNITS

Thinking of the two garments as one unit will help save time rethreading and changing serger settings.

Plan to join as many seams as possible, assembly-line fashion, chaining each new seam without cutting the chain between sections, before moving on to detailed areas.

Likewise, when working with bands of joined laces or trims, save time by assembling one long continuous strip of joined laces, then apply and trim to garment measurements as required.

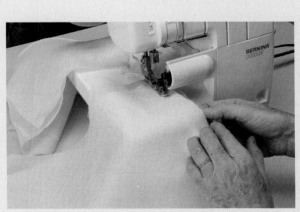

The sides of the tap pants can be serged in series without cutting thread or pausing between sections.

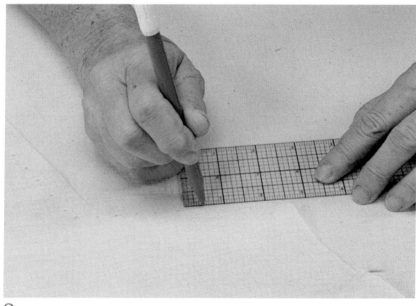

2 *Mark the seamline with a water-soluble marker.*

Prepare the bust points: Starch the camisole and lightly mark the seamline on the right side of the fabric with a water-soluble fabric marker **(2)**.

Cut a tiny square from the point of the seam allowance over the left bust, aligning one corner of the cutout with the apex of the point. Cut a similar square from the right-bust seam allowance. Further trim the seam allowance to 3mm for 2 in. on the underarm side of the right-bust point apex. The trimmed area will resemble an L shape.

Prepare the center front: Slash the seam allowance to the seam line at center front. Spread the slashed seam allowance flat so the raw edge forms a straight line between the two points, allowing the rest of the fabric to radiate out from the slash and form a large fold below it.

Cut a strip of the lace assembly to equal the point-to-point line plus 4 in., aligning the center of the lace pattern with the slash at center front **(3)**.

Conventionally staystitch the lace to the camisole as you did to the leg opening. To ensure that the stitching area is clear at the beginning and end of the seam, make an "airplane fold"—fold the

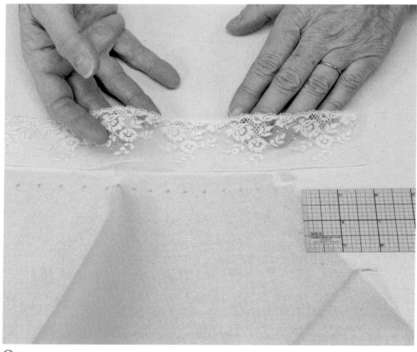

3 *Prepare the top edge of the camisole by marking the seamline, trimming, and centering the lace pattern.*

ends of the lace and underarm side of the left bust-point seam allowance away from the bust-point cutouts at a 45° angle **(4)**. Stabilize the fold with artist's tape or pins.

Similarly, return to the serger to roll-hem the lace to the camisole between the bust points **(5)**. To roll-hem the lace to the camisole at the serger, increase cutting width to 3mm and set the machine for roll hemming. Lift the presser foot and position the needle carefully at the beginning of the seam over the left bust point, being sure not to stitch through the header of the lace that extends beyond the fabric. Use similar caution at the end of the seam.

Again, press the hem toward the lace so the header of the lace remains flat and fabric rolls over it in a receiving hem.

To trim the underarm and back of the camisole, close the remaining side seam and restarch the camisole and final strip of the lace assembly. Pin the lace around the back and underarms of the camisole top from bust point to bust point, centering the pattern at center back and allowing the ends of the lace to extend over the previously stitched center portion.

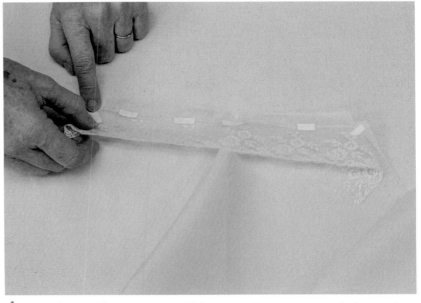

4 *After clipping the center, spread the camisole top in a straight line and tape the lace into position.*

5 *Roll-hem the lace to the camisole between bust points. Fold the ends of the lace out of the way so you won't stitch them into the seam allowance.*

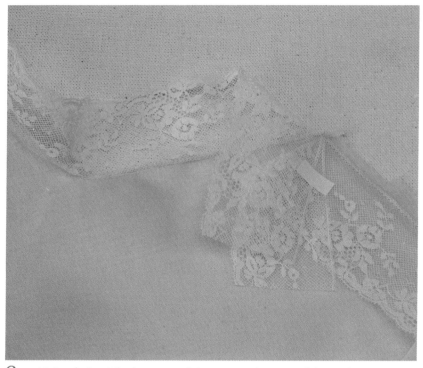

Again, staystitch the lace from bust point to bust point around the back and underarm of the top. Fold the fabric and lace out of the way at the apex of each corner **(6),** as you did previously.

Return to the serger, clear the stitch fingers and raise the presser foot and needle. Position the apex of the left bust-point cutout directly under the needle with the L portion of the cutout flush against the inside of the lower knife blade **(7).** Serge the hem lace to the camisole as before, being careful not to stitch through the header of lace at the end of the seam over the right bust point.

To miter the corners at the center front, press all hems toward the lace, arranging excess lace at the center into a fold so the fold line extends vertically upward beyond the center front of the camisole **(8).**

6 *Fold the ends of the lace out of the way at the start of the underarm seam on both sides of the corner so they won't be caught in the stitching.*

8 *Miter the corners at center front, pressing the lace so the fold lines are vertical.*

7 *With the stitch fingers cleared, position the folded lace at the start of the underarm seam under the needle with the L portion of the cutout flush with the inside of the lower knife blade.*

To finish the bust points, lap the ends of the lace over each other, again positioning the fold to extend vertically above the bust point. Starting at the fabric edge and working to the outside, use the conventional machine to edgestitch the miters in a tiny zigzag hairline seam. (Loosening the upper-thread tension and decreasing the stitch length will allow the stitches to sink into the lace and disappear.)

Using very sharp embroidery scissors, trim excess lace close to the zigzag stitching **(9).**

To make straps for the camisole, thread ribbon through lace beading. Trace the outline of the bust points onto the beading assembly and overcast the outline.

Pin the prepared strap to the camisole, matching the center of the beading to the center of the bust point and the flatlocked edge to the inner edge of the roll hem. Edgestitch in the ditch to secure, and hand-tack the lace to the strap at the point. Try on the camisole to adjust the length of the strap before finishing the back edge of the strap and securing it to the camisole.

Embellish the center front of the camisole with a ribbon bow, which can be made by looping ribbon around the spindles of the serger. Pass the free end around behind the loops and tie in front. Remove the bow from the spindles and trim the ends diagonally **(10).**

Press the elastic-casing allowance into an S-shaped fold at the top of the pants, as described on p. 52.

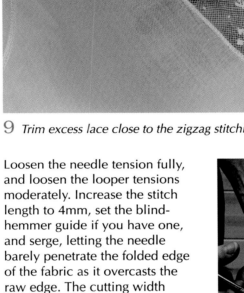

9 *Trim excess lace close to the zigzag stitching.*

Loosen the needle tension fully, and loosen the looper tensions moderately. Increase the stitch length to 4mm, set the blind-hemmer guide if you have one, and serge, letting the needle barely penetrate the folded edge of the fabric as it overcasts the raw edge. The cutting width should be normal to support over-casting. Open the fold and press flat. Fill the casing with elastic.

Return the serger to bias-hairline settings, and close the final seam at center back and crotch.

Don't try to finish lace or ribbon edges with a roll hem. The lace threads are too far apart, patterned areas are too irregular for a smooth hem, and ribbons are just too bulky to roll well. Instead, flatlock the raw edge of ribbon or lace with a narrow cutting width and a small stitch length.

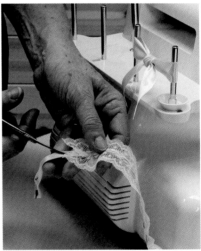

10 *Tie a decorative bow for the front of the camisole and trim the ends of the beaded lace.*

When sewing lace, ribbon, or other prefinished edges, rotate the upper knife out of position to remove any danger of accidentally trimming the edge, and stitch as usual.

Photo Index

This photo index will help you to review and compare serger seams and finishes, and to locate them in the book. You will see at a glance various treatments you can use, grouped under five headings: basics, hems, utility and decorative stitches, specialty stitches, and complete projects. Where appropriate, photos are accompanied by a chart with the serger settings that produced the stitch.

Basics

BASIC FOUR-THREAD SERGED SEAM

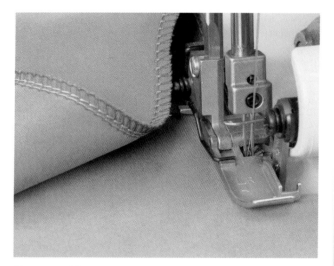

NEEDLES/ LOOPERS	THREAD	TENSION
Left needle	Garment thread	Normal
Right needle	Garment thread	Normal
Upper looper	Garment thread	Normal
Lower looper	Garment thread	Normal
SERGER SETTINGS		
Stitch length	Normal (2mm to 3mm)	
Cutting width	Normal for fabric	
Differential feed	Normal	

See page 56.

NEEDLES/ LOOPERS	THREAD	TENSION
Left needle	Garment thread	Normal
Right needle	Garment thread	Normal
Upper looper	Woolly nylon	Balanced
Lower looper	Woolly nylon	Balanced

SERGER SETTINGS

Stitch length	3mm to 3.5mm
Cutting width	Balance to weight of fabric
Differential feed	Normal unless fabric waves
Optional settings	Use roll-hem setting for light knits

FOUR-THREAD SEAM FOR LIGHTWEIGHT KNITS

See the discussion of overstitching, which begins on page 51.

NEEDLES/ LOOPERS	THREAD	TENSION
Left needle	Omit (for wider seams, thread the left needle and omit the right)	
Right needle	Garment thread	Normal
Upper looper	Garment thread	Normal
Lower looper	Garment thread	Normal

SERGER SETTINGS

Stitch length	Normal (2mm to 3mm)
Cutting width	Normal for fabric
Differential feed	Normal unless fabric puckers

BASIC THREE-THREAD SEAM

See page 56.

TWO-THREAD ROLLED SEAM

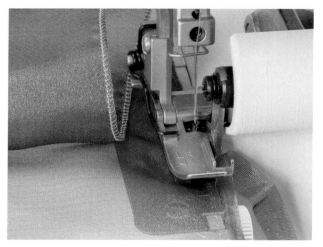

See page 57.

NEEDLES/ LOOPERS	THREAD	TENSION
Left needle	Omit	
Right needle	Garment thread	Normal
Upper looper	Bypass	
Lower looper	Clear nylon	High

SERGER SETTINGS	
Stitch length	2mm to 2.5mm
Cutting width	Widest (3mm)
Differential feed	Normal unless fabric puckers
Optional settings	Adjust serger for roll hemming; for three-thread rolled seam, thread upper looper with clear nylon under high tension.

TWO-THREAD SEAM FOR JOINING LACE

See page 91.

NEEDLES/ LOOPERS	THREAD	TENSION
Left needle	Omit	
Right needle	Garment thread	Normal
Upper looper	Bypass	
Lower looper	Garment thread	Normal

SERGER SETTINGS	
Stitch length	2mm
Cutting width	Disengage upper knife
Differential feed	.07 to prevent curling
Optional settings	Adjust serger for roll hemming

NEEDLES/ LOOPERS	THREAD	TENSION
Left needle	Omit	
Right needle	Garment thread	Normal
Upper looper	Bypass	
Lower looper	Woolly nylon	High

SERGER SETTINGS	
Stitch length	2.5mm to 3mm
Cutting width	Narrowest (1mm)
Differential feed	Normal unless fabric puckers
Optional settings	Adjust serger for roll hemming

FRENCH SEAM

See page 58.

Hems

NEEDLES/ LOOPERS	THREAD	TENSION
Left needle	Omit	
Right needle	Garment thread	Normal
Upper looper	Garment thread	Normal
Lower looper	Garment thread	Normal

SERGER SETTINGS	
Stitch length	Normal (2mm to 3mm)
Cutting width	Normal for fabric
Differential feed	Above normal for easing, or normal

EASED OVERLOCK HEM

See page 61.

BASIC ROLLED HEM

See page 62.

NEEDLES/ LOOPERS	THREAD	TENSION
Left needle	Omit	
Right needle	Garment thread	Normal
Upper looper	Lightweight, such as two-ply poly	Normal
Lower looper	Woolly nylon	High
SERGER SETTINGS		
Stitch length	2mm to 2.5mm	
Cutting width	Wide	
Differential feed	Normal unless fabric puckers	
Optional settings	Adjust serger for roll hemming	

ROLLED RECEIVING HEM

See page 62.

NEEDLES/ LOOPERS	THREAD	TENSION
Left needle	Omit	
Right needle	Garment thread	Normal
Upper looper	Woolly nylon	High
Lower looper	Woolly nylon	High
SERGER SETTINGS		
Stitch length	To suit fabric	
Cutting width	Widest (3mm)	
Differential feed	Normal unless fabric puckers	
Optional settings	Adjust serger for roll hemming	

NEEDLES/ LOOPERS	THREAD	TENSION
Left needle	Omit	
Right needle	Harmonizing	Normal
Upper looper	Woolly nylon	Normal
Lower looper	Woolly nylon	Fairly high

SERGER SETTINGS	
Stitch length	2mm
Cutting width	Normal for fabric
Differential feed	.07 below normal to pull fabric

LETTUCE-EDGE HEM

See page 63.

NEEDLES/ LOOPERS	THREAD	TENSION
Left needle	Omit	
Right needle	To suit coverage	Normal
Upper looper	To suit coverage	Balanced
Lower looper	To suit coverage	High

SERGER SETTINGS	
Stitch length	2mm
Cutting width	Widest (3mm)
Differential feed	Normal unless fabric puckers
Optional settings	Adjust serger for roll hemming

MONOFILAMENT HEM

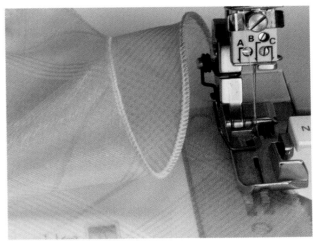

See page 82.

BLIND HEM

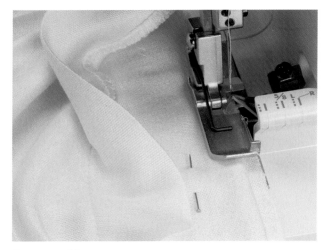

See page 63.

NEEDLES/ LOOPERS	THREAD	TENSION
Left needle	Garment thread	Fairly low
Right needle	Omit	
Upper looper	Garment thread	Slightly low
Lower looper	Garment thread	Fairly high

SERGER SETTINGS	
Stitch length	Medium to long
Cutting width	Normal
Differential feed	Normal

Utility and Decorative Stitches

NEEDLES/ LOOPERS	THREAD	TENSION
Left needle	Omit	
Right needle	Garment thread	Normal
Upper looper	Garment thread	Normal
Lower looper	Garment thread	Normal

SERGER SETTINGS	
Stitch length	2.5mm to 3mm
Cutting width	Normal for fabric
Differential feed	Normal

SINGLE-LAYER OVERCASTING

See page 60.

NEEDLES/ LOOPERS	THREAD	TENSION
Left needle	Omit	
Right needle	Garment thread	Normal
Upper looper	Woolly nylon	Balanced
Lower looper	Woolly nylon	Balanced

SERGER SETTINGS	
Stitch length	1.5mm to 2mm for coverage
Cutting width	Balance to weight of fabric
Differential feed	Normal unless fabric puckers

MOCK HONG KONG FINISH

See page 77.

BASIC TUCKS

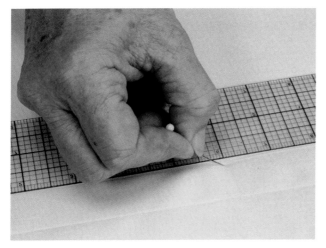

See pages 70-72.

NEEDLES/ LOOPERS	THREAD	TENSION
Left needle	Omit	
Right needle	Garment thread	Normal
Upper looper	Bypass	
Lower looper	Garment thread	Normal

SERGER SETTINGS	
Stitch length	3mm
Cutting width	Balance to weight of fabric
Differential feed	.07
Optional settings	Use roll-hem setting for light knits

DECORATIVE TUCKS

See pages 70-72.

NEEDLES/ LOOPERS	THREAD	TENSION
Left needle	Garment thread	Normal
Right needle	Garment thread	Normal
Upper looper	Decorative thread	High
Lower looper	Garment thread	Low

SERGER SETTINGS	
Stitch length	Moderatelly dense (2mm)
Cutting width	Balance to weight of fabric
Differential feed	.07
Optional settings	Use roll-hem setting for very narrow tucks; use edge-stitching attachment to help control fold line

NEEDLES/ LOOPERS	THREAD	TENSION
Left needle	Garment thread	Fairly low
Right needle	Omit	
Upper looper	Woolly nylon	Slightly low
Lower looper	Contrast	Fairly high

SERGER SETTINGS	
Stitch length	Medium (adjust so nylon fluffs up)
Cutting width	Narrowest (1mm)
Differential feed	Normal

DECORATIVE FLATLOCKING

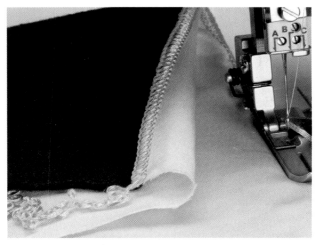

See pages 58 and 73.

NEEDLES/ LOOPERS	THREAD	TENSION
Left needle	Garment or accent thread	Normal
Right needle	Garment or accent thread	Normal
Upper looper	Decorative thread	Low
Lower looper	Garment or accent thread	High

SERGER SETTINGS	
Stitch length	Increase so trim will not bunch up on stitch fingers
Cutting width	Balance to weight of fabric
Differential feed	.07

DECORATIVE CHAINING

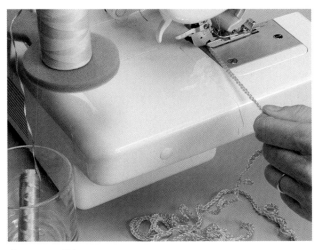

See page 74.

Specialty Stitches

Sewing Elastic
See pages 52-53.

Gathering
See page 54.

Plackets
See page 48.

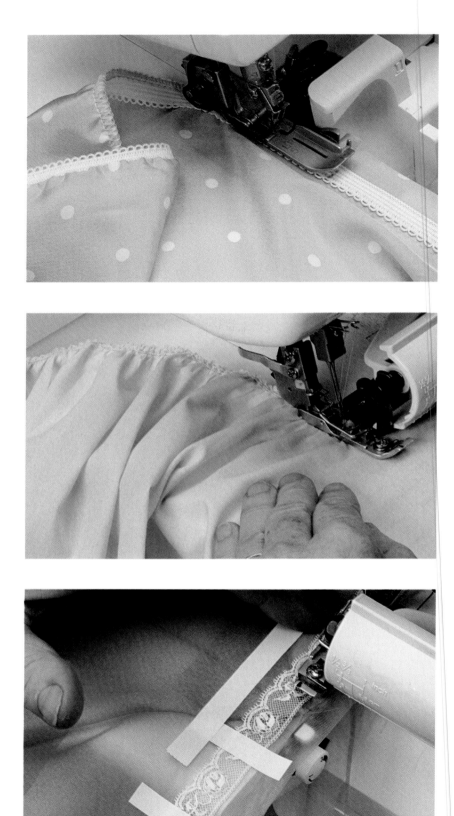

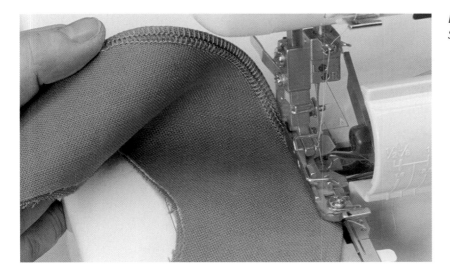

Decorative Edging
See page 73.

Metallic Thread-Traced Hem
See pages 79-80.

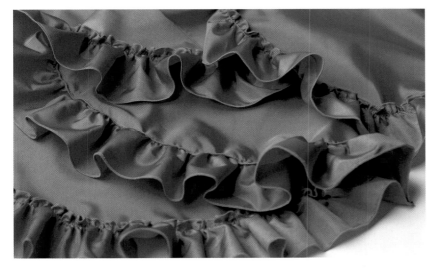

Gathered Ruffles
See page 83.

Complete Projects

Quick Scarf
See page 89.

Quick Cowl Neck
See page 67.

Quick Eyeglass Case
See page 76.

Quick Hair Ornament
See page 81.

Camisole and Tap Pants
See pages 90-95.

Elegant Silk Knit Top
See pages 67-69.

Index

Look for these and other *Threads* books at
your local bookstore or sewing retailer.

For a catalog of the complete line of *Threads* books and videos, write to
The Taunton Press, P.O. Box 5506, Newtown, CT 06470-5506.